Possum Hollow

Book 1

Possum Hollow

Book 1

Levi B. Weber

Herald
Press

Scottdale, Pennsylvania
Waterloo, Ontario

Library of Congress Cataloging-in-Publication Data
Weber, Levi B., 1911-
  Possum hollow / Levi B. Weber
    p. cm.
  ISBN 0-8361-9126-9 (bk. 1 : alk. paper)
    1. Weber, Levi B., 1911—Childhood and youth. 2. Farm
  life—Pennsylvania—Lancaster County. 3. Farm life—
  Virginia—Amelia County. 4. Mennonites—Pennsylvania—
  Lancaster County—Biography. 5. Amelia County (Va.)—
  Biography. 6. Lancaster County (Pa.)—Biography. I. Title.
CT275.W3526 A3 2001
974.8′15044—dc21

                                          00-053940

The paper used in this publication is recycled and meets the minimum
requirements of American National Standard for Information
Sciences—Permanence of Paper for Printed Library Materials, ANSI
Z39.48-1984.

POSSUM HOLLOW, BOOK 1
Copyright © 2001 by Herald Press, Scottdale, Pa. 15683
  Published simultaneously in Canada by Herald Press,
  Waterloo, Ont. N2L 6H7. All rights reserved
Library of Congress Catalog Card Number: 00-053940
International Standard Book Number: 0-8361-9126-9
Printed in the United States of America
Book and cover design by Jim Butti
Cover and inside illustrations by Joy Dunn Keenan
Amelia maps by Suzanne Hinson

10 09 08 07 06 05 04 03 02 01 10 9 8 7 6 5 4 3 2 1

To order or request information, please call 1-800-759-4447 (individu-
als); 1-800-245-7894 (trade). Website: www.mph.org

To my wife,
June Elizabeth Weber

Without the encouragement I received from June, I would never have written *Possum Hollow*. When she heard me tell stories to the children, she would often say, "Why don't you write about it?"

She knew it wouldn't be easy because she had written a book, *The Tribe of Jacob*, stories about her mother's family of fifteen children growing up in the Shenandoah Valley of Virginia.

June was always glad to read my manuscripts and suggest corrections or changes before they were given to the typist. Thank you, June!

Contents

Preface. *9*

Getting Things Together. **11**
    1. Early Memories 13
    2. Burned Out! 17
    3. Playing Robinson Crusoe 21
    4. "December's as Pleasant as May" 26

Beginning to Learn **31**
    5. Esty's Failed Plan. 34
    6. Corn Dale 37
    7. Building the New House. 40
    8. Mr. Maxie 44
    9. Mary Ella 47
    10. The Heatwole Flower 52
    11. Charlie Wallace and Lost Honor. 57

Doing Things **61**
    12. Elements of Self-Expression 63
    13. Eva 69
    14. The "Funny Thing" 73
    15. The Copperhead. 76
    16. Then the Chimney Burned 81
    17. Flory's New Shoes 86

School and Possums **91**

    18. Mishoos. 93
    19. Mama's Trip 96
    20. About Possums 102
    21. The Echo. 107
    22. Mary Elizabeth 111

Pennsylvania, Here We Come! **115**

    23. Going Home Again 117
    24. Some Days Are Like That 121
    25. Emmalene. 127
    26. Don't Pass the Elderberry Pie! 132
    27. How, What, When, and Where? 140

The Author 142

Preface

The stories my family told about the old days were so interesting that I always wished I had been there too. That's why in later years I began to write about my own childhood near a little village in southern Virginia.

Pleasant memories are easy to recall. My "kindergarten" was meadows, streams, birds, and flowers. My brother and sisters were my teachers. Papa and Mama enjoyed watching our games and activities, only imposing restraints when we went beyond accepted rules. Those youthful ways changed when we moved from that quiet southern community to busy Lancaster County, Pennsylvania.

When a few of my short stories appeared in our local school and church monthly magazine, some of my friends suggested that I write a book about those days. So that's what I did. The earliest event in the stories is my parents' marriage day in 1897. The final event is a hundred years later, August 1997, at our family reunion near Lancaster, Pennsylvania.

I have named this series of books *Possum Hollow.* This is the first volume.

I wish to acknowledge several people who were

helpful to me in writing these stories. My wife, June, carefully read all my manuscripts, correcting spelling and offering helpful suggestions. My typist, Susan Wilmoth, typed all my stories, keeping them cataloged and stored in her computer. I also thank many others who encouraged me to write.

—*Levi B. Weber*
 Newport News, Virginia

Getting Things Together

1

Early Memories

Our family never sat down to talk about old times like some of our friends did. Our group conversations were more about things that had to be done or about ideas and plans for the future. But I always wanted to know more about what had happened around home before I was born and before I was old enough to remember.

There didn't seem to be an effort to avoid the past but rather an active interest in what we were doing now. However, the occasional remarks about the past—from Papa and Mama and the older children—stirred my imagination. I wanted to know more about the beginnings of our family. I guess that's why I was called "nosy" by the rest of the family. The term was not necessarily negative or unfriendly. That's just the way I was.

Papa never talked about his early youth or his short service in the army. His few remarks were about his father and mother. Mama spoke a bit about her school days and some things about our earlier days as a family. Eva, the oldest child, shared some things about her early years when Grandpa Weber, in his old age, lived with us.

Those stories and others I heard along the way—happenings before I was born, some pleasant and some tragic—formed a community of history in my mind. Each tidbit I heard found its niche in the bigger story. It seemed that, way back there, I too was a part of the family. So I tell what I heard and later what I myself experienced.

Eva remembered our home at Oakalone near Farmersville in Lancaster County, Pennsylvania. Grandpa Weber lived with my family and had his own separate room. Eva said, "I would visit Grandpa there almost every day. I was five years old, and he would let me sit on his lap while he carefully peeled an apple. The peel was thin and stayed in one long, curling piece. Grandpa would cut off a slice of apple for me and tell me a story as we ate the apple together."

Grandpa had been a country preacher, and for a living he made all kinds of wooden farm tools and baskets. Eva told me, "Grandpa made a neat little chest of drawers for my very own. When I was six or seven years old, he died. I missed him very much and could hardly be comforted."

My parents had four children at Oakalone: Eva, Helen, Franklin, and Esther. Times were hard everywhere, and it took a long time to save just a little money, especially on a small farm with children to clothe, feed, and raise. The years passed. By 1909 they had been married twelve years.

Papa used to say, "Mom, I guess we'll have to move to Virginia. I hear land is cheap down there."

She didn't think much about it until one day he came in the front door. "I'm going to look at some property below Richmond," he said. Two days later he took the train to Petersburg, Virginia.

While he was gone, Mama cried when she was not around the children. She worked hard at a lot of things that really didn't need doing. At night her dreams were gloomy and foreboding.

In about a week, Mama had a letter from Papa: "Meet me at the railroad station in Lancaster on Saturday. Since that's market day, you'll be in town anyway."

The minute she saw her husband, she knew that he had made a decision of some kind, but he did not seem to want to talk about it right away. So she told him how many eggs the chickens had laid while he had been gone and how well the children had behaved. "Look," she said, "we sold almost five dollars' worth of eggs and potatoes today. I know if we work hard, we can make it right here."

He still wasn't ready to talk about the trip. Then, edging a little closer to the subject, she asked, "Did your socks and shirts last the trip?"

"Yes, you packed my suitcase just right."

Finally, she could not stand it any longer. "Did you find a place you like?"

"Yes."

"Well, Henry, why don't you tell me about it."

So he did. "I've found a little farm at Chesterfield, near Petersburg. It looked good, and I signed a contract to buy it. We'll move in a couple months."

The news stunned the family. Moving so far away was frightening.

When Granny, Mama's mother, was told, she exclaimed in Pennsylvania German, "Mary, *fer was wit du zu Virginny geh* (why do you want to go to Virginia)?"

Mama didn't want to go, and the children didn't want to leave Oakalone. But they all trusted Papa. As the family prepared to move, it became an adventure. When moving time came, leaving Oakalone was a bit easier.

Friends and relatives helped to load the farm tools and household belongings on the train at the Lancaster rail siding. The cow and two horses went in the cattle car. It was a mixed-car train, so the family went along in one of the passenger cars.

As the train began to slowly move and juggle to the main track, Papa said, "Well, here we are moving on to Chester, all aboard with nothing left behind."

Mama replied, "Yes, nothing except our friends and relatives."

2

Burned Out!

About a year later, Mama was stirring apple butter on the stove. The family was in their own house on their own little farm near Chester, between Richmond and Petersburg. The farmhouse was back a lane lined with trees and bushes. It had two stories with steep gables and a large fireplace chimney at one end. Papa had fixed screens and a screen door so Mama could keep flies out of the kitchen.

Mama was almost happy. She began to sing as she stirred. Every day the little farm began to feel more like home. From the window she could see the barn with the cow standing in the barnyard and the chicken house nearby. It was late summer. The big girls were outside watching over the little ones at play. Papa was working out in the field. Things seemed good.

She also had begun to have that mysterious feeling of ownership that women experience when they are carrying a child. The new family member would be born in the spring. Mama sang as she went out the door for more wood. Then she saw it—a wisp of smoke and a little tongue of flame coming from the gable end of the house beside the chimney.

Mama ran as fast as she could to the field, calling, "Henry, Henry, the house is on fire!"

As soon as Papa heard, he came running to the house, shouting toward the neighbors, "Fire! Fire!"

It all happened so fast. Neighbors came running and began to throw things out of the house. The fire was too high for them to get buckets of water up to it, and there were no pressure hoses. Mama could not grasp the finality of it and hoped that somehow it wasn't true. She saw the open screen door and thought about flies.

People were just tossing things out of the windows. Mason jars of fruit came bouncing on the ground, smashing to pieces. The sewing machine was just inside the door, but no one got it out. Then the whole house suddenly burst into flames, and everybody fled to a safe distance. The fire was too fierce and hot for them to do anything more.

Little five-year-old Brother (Franklin) was fascinated. He kept watching to see the brick chimney fall, but it stayed standing there, with the dying flames and smoke swirling around it. Eva was crying. Her little chest of drawers from her grandpa was gone. No one had brought it out.

When Papa first saw the flames licking up the side of the house, he knew it was lost. He rounded up the four children and ran out the lane with them to a safe distance. Papa told twelve-year-old Eva,

"You be sure to keep the children here. I don't want you to get hurt. The house can be replaced, but children can't be."

Then he joined the others, who were dragging things out of the house.

The fire burned with a frenzy, and it was soon over. Little had been saved. Papa put the girls to work at their familiar evening farm chores. Then he went to Mama and the little ones where they were looking dejectedly at the scattered remnants of their furniture.

"Look, Henry," Mama said. "There's the sewing machine. I thought it was burned."

"Why, no," he reminded her, "you dragged it out yourself the last minute. I was afraid you would stumble and hurt yourself. Now you take care. I don't want anything to happen to you."

The neighbors expressed their sympathy, and several of the men offered to return later and help with the cleanup and rebuilding. Some of them even offered to give us temporary lodging. But Papa said, "Thanks, but we'll make do somehow. After all, we still have the barn for shelter."

The sun was getting low in the sky, so the neighbors went home to do their chores. Then the family was alone, looking at the last of the fire slowly burning on the floor, popping now and then, throwing sparks. The acrid smell of burned clothing hung in the air.

Mama tried to figure what to have for supper, but she had no stove. She had learned to cook at her childhood home when she was so small that she needed to stand on a stool to reach the pan. Her stove had always been the place of retreat. She could think better there.

Papa was walking around what was left of the house. A tear ran down one cheek. He wiped it off with the back of his hand. Then he started for the barn to do the evening chores and told the girls to gather the eggs.

Mama took the little ones to her side and began to look for some jars that had not broken. Then, as an utter misfit, the rooster crowed. What had Granny always said? "When a rooster crows in the evening, it is a sign of bad luck." Or was it good luck? What difference did it make?

<u>3</u>

Playing Robinson Crusoe

The girls hurried through their work and went to join the others. Papa was always the strong one in the family. Mama looked at him wistfully, hoping to see some hint of encouragement. But even he felt empty.

"We can all be thankful that no one was hurt. We saved what we could, and we still have the barn and shed. Now let's play Robinson Crusoe and see how clever we can be with what we have left."

His words began to stir up his own courage. "We'll fix up a place in the barn to sleep, and Mom will try to find something for supper. If we all work together, things will come out all right. Tomorrow is another day. We'll face it when it comes."

Time dragged along in step with a grudging series of makeshift efforts to keep life going. The

shed was divided into two rooms for living space. The kitchen range was salvaged and installed at one end. The family used some of the furniture and stored the remaining few pieces in the barn.

With forced cheerfulness, Papa declared, "Well, here is our new little house."

Then something totally unexpected gave them new hope. As word of the tragedy got around the community, people began to bring gifts of clothing and canned things. There were offers of help. The sawmill man brought a two-horse wagonload of lumber and unloaded it by the barn.

Our neighbors did all that with a natural and open kindness, without attaching any hint of obligation or assigning blame for the fire. No one said what should have been done or what might not have been done. No one even said, "You don't have to pay for it. Just help us sometime."

Never before had Papa experienced such freedom in giving and receiving. It was new and refreshing. They knew they could build again. There was a start with the lumber, and they also received notice of a small insurance settlement.

Mama was relieved. She couldn't face the thought of a baby being born in the shed.

Then Helen got sick. It began with headache and nausea. As it developed into fever and aching muscles, the doctor gave her a strong iron tonic. "It's good for rheumatism," he assured her.

Helen cried herself through the ordeal. Her right leg was paralyzed. The doctor said, "It's probably infantile paralysis."

The family felt deeply for the little eight-year-old

SUN
12 *Mamie, 19...*
to Richard X

MON
13 *Grandpa R...
to Richard*

TUE
14 *Sun is shining*

WED
15 *Sugar bringing...
very cold...
out to the...*

THU
16 *we were at Ri...
X*

FRI
17 *I was old...*

SAT
18 *...*

MARCH 1911

*...where at
...back...
...back round*

*August
at school*

SUN
19

MON
20

TUE
21

*I went to walk...
...it ches for 22 weeks*

WED
22

*grandma's
sick*

THU
23

*we have a little
baby brother*

FRI
24

*Tomorrow we
are going to*

SAT
25

Levi

girl crippled by polio (as we call it now). Papa almost cried when he thought about it. He gave her a little pocket-sized diary, and she began to write in it:

Jan. 1	I cannot walk without crutches.
Jan. 3	I sewed on the sewing machine.
Jan. 5	The capenders [sic] came.
Jan. 11	We got the weatherboarding on the house.
Jan. 13	I sewed Mama's apron but it got pretty crooked.
Jan. 27	Papa was in town with 43 doz. eggs.
Feb. 14	Franklin took castor oil.
Feb. 26	I finished Elsie Dinsmore.
Mar. 9	Lessie Wenger came.
Mar. 22	I must walk on crutches 22 weeks.
Mar. 23	Mama is sick.
Mar. 24	We have a new baby brother.

I was that little boy who came with the spring. My parents named me Levi, after Papa's younger brother, a minister in the Reformed Church in Coatesville, Pennsylvania. We were then a family of five children: Eva, Helen, Brother (Franklin), Esty (Esther) and Baby (Levi).

Things were back to normal again. But Papa was deeply disturbed by all that had happened during the last year. He wasn't happy, and it bothered him. Mama could read his mood by the way he went about his work. She was restless, too, and kept extra busy. Something seemed to be missing and unfinished, and she couldn't talk to Papa about it.

4

"December's as Pleasant as May"

The trauma of the fire gradually faded as new hope grew into new expectation. The smell of new paint overcame the harsh smell of burned wood and fabric. Helen went to Richmond once a week to be treated by an osteopath.

Then Brother fell, cut his tongue, and required surgery. Papa couldn't understand why the events of the last year embarrassed him. He even felt some personal responsibility and guilt.

Pondering these things, his mind went back to the years when he first met Mama. They both grew up in large Mennonite families. Papa's father was a preacher in an Old Order church. Neither he nor his brothers and sister stayed with that church.

When Papa grew up, he enlisted in the army and served three years in the Utah Territory. After that service, he returned to his home community. Although he had only a country-school education, he took some summer classes and qualified to teach. In his school at Bird-in-Hand, Pennsylvania, he taught a class in German reading, since many of his pupils were Amish.

During that time he met saucy little Mary Ann Burkholder (Mama) at a Sunday school picnic. He was amused at the way she could switch from speaking fluent Pennsylvania German to proper English during conversation. They were married later that year (1897).

He was twenty-seven years old, and she was nineteen. Neither was a Christian, but soon after they were married, Mama accepted Christ and became a member of the Mennonite Church. Her father was a Mennonite, but her mother was raised among the Dunkard Brethren.

Papa was a taciturn philosopher. He quoted bits of wisdom that were rules of life. "Contentment is a state of mind and not of circumstances." "Work hard, be honest, do the best you can, and things will work out." "Don't worry; tomorrow is another day."

He was influenced by a song they sang in the Pike Church when he was a boy. It is on page 300 in the *Gesang-Buch.*

Richtet euch selbst allezeit.
[Set a watch on yourself all the time.]

Its theme was watchful living and self-denial. Such a life held no fear. The song ends,

Wer sich selbst richt't hier auf Erden,
Dem darf dort nicht bange werden.
[Whoever watches oneself here on earth,
Will not need to be afraid yonder.]

There was no Mennonite congregation in Chester, and Mama wanted to do something about it. She had an idea. Papa said, "Go ahead and see what you can do about starting a church."

None of the local churches would offer her any space. They thought she was "a Catholic or something," because of her plain Mennonite clothing. Papa was sometimes referred to as the man whose wife was a nun. Finally the school said she could use a room, if she paid for the lamp oil. She used some of her egg money and made a deal.

Mama sent a note to the *Gospel Herald:*

We have been blessed with an opportunity to hold services in a hall in Chester, Va., on Oct. 31, Nov. 1 and 2. Pray for us—etc. Mary A. Weber

Mama talked to the girls about it. A bishop was coming to preach, a man from Denbigh called "George R." The girls knew Papa did not "belong to church." Helen, in one of their little talks with Mama, said maybe they should pray for Papa. Eva, with characteristic loyalty, rather sharply interjected that they had enough to pray about for themselves.

Papa never had heard things explained just like the tall blond Brunk said them. He was deeply touched and later said, "Now I know what it means to be sinsick!"

Mama's prayers were answered. Not only was Papa baptized, but so were Eva and Helen. Papa's old anxiety was gone. He began to sing at his work. A favorite song was from the *Methodist Hymnal.*

How tedious and tasteless the hours,
    when Jesus no longer I see—,
But when I am happy in Him,
    December's as pleasant as May.

Our family agreed that we wanted to live in a Mennonite community. We sold the little farm in Chester. During a short stay in Denbigh (near Newport News), we lived near Young's Mill. Then we moved to Amelia, about thirty-five miles southwest of Richmond. It was about 1912, and I was a toddler.

There Papa went into the building business. Almost a year to the day after Mama had written to the *Gospel Herald* from Chester, Papa wrote from Amelia that Brother George R. Brunk was coming to Amelia to officiate at communion services.

In the space of two years, my family's world turned around. The house had burned, Helen's right leg was paralyzed, a new house was built, a baby was born, Brother was hurt, Papa and the older girls became Christians, the farm was sold, we stayed several months in Denbigh, and then we settled in Amelia!

It was a new start, with a strong Christian home. To everyone, "December . . . [was] as pleasant as May!"

Beginning
to Learn

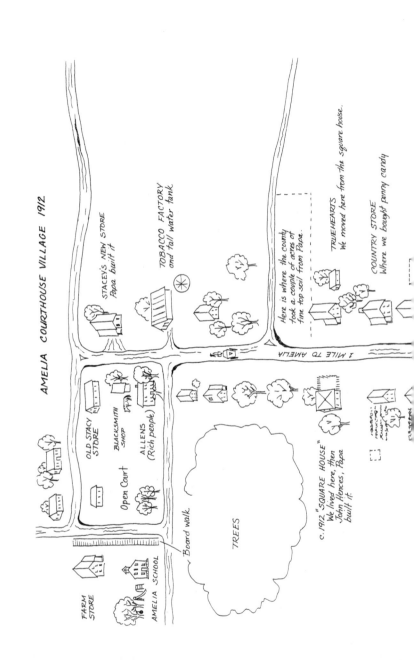

AMELIA COURTHOUSE VILLAGE 1912

FARM STORE

AMELIA SCHOOL

OLD STACY STORE

Open Court

BLACKSMITH SHOP

ALLENS (Rich people)

STACEY'S NEW STORE
Papa built it

TOBACCO FACTORY
and tall water tank

Board walk

TREES

c. 1912 "SQUARE HOUSE"
We lived here, then
John Hexces, Papa
built it.

1 MILE TO AMELIA

Here is where the county
took a couple of acres of
fine top soil from Papa.

TRUEHEARTS
We moved here from the square house.

COUNTRY STORE
Where we bought penny candy

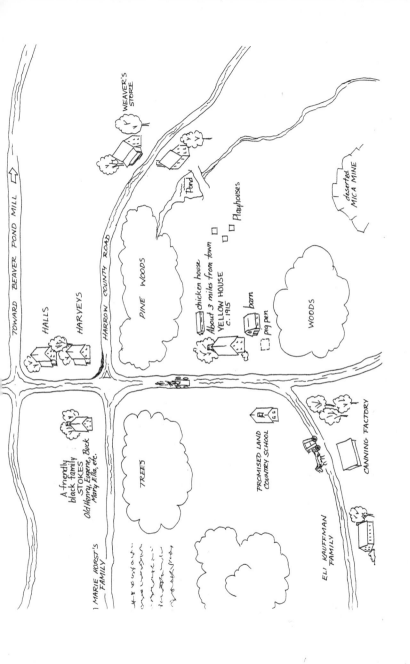

TOWARD BEAVER POND MILL →

WEAVER'S STORE

HALLS

HARVEYS

HARROW COUNTY ROAD

PINE WOODS

Pond

Playhouses

A friendly
black family
STOKES
Old Henry, Eugene, Buck
Mary Ella, etc.

chicken house
About 3 miles from town
YELLOW HOUSE
c. 1915

barn

pig pen

deserted
MICA MINE

WOODS

TREES

MARIE HORST'S FAMILY

PROMISED LAND
COUNTRY SCHOOL

CANNING FACTORY

ELI KAUFFMAN
FAMILY

5

Esty's Failed Plan

One of the first things I can remember after moving to Amelia is John Hentz's dog, a little terrier named Tilly.

We lived in a house we called Truehart's, after the people who used to live there. Even though I had been successfully potty trained, I was still called Baby at three and a half years of age.

Right across the narrow road from us was the Square House. That was where the John Hentzes lived. Papa had built it and sold it to them. A neat picket fence enclosed their front yard.

They had no children so they gave us a lot of their attention. Mr. Hentz made us a little wooden sled to pull around, even when there was no snow.

What Esty and I liked most was going with Mama to visit Mrs. Hentz. We would sit on the floor and play with Tilly while they talked. As we left, Mrs. Hentz usually gave each of us a piece of candy.

She explained to us that they kept Tilly in the house when they were home. But if they were gone, they put Tilly in the yard so she could keep strangers away.

One day when the older children were at school, Mama left Esty and me at home while she went across the road to visit. She told six-year-old Esty, "Don't let Baby go out on the road."

When Mrs. Hentz greeted Mama at the door, Tilly slipped out and settled in the shade by the porch.

As soon as Mama left, Esty said, "If we play in our front yard, maybe Mrs. Hentz will see us and invite us over for candy." We made a lot of noise as we played, but the plan didn't work.

Then Esty cooked up another idea: "If you wander over there alone 'by mistake,' maybe Mrs. Hentz will invite you in and give you some candy for both of us. I don't think Mama would care."

Esty started me across the road. But just before I reached their gate, I heard her say softly, "Baby, come on back." I went back.

Then she sent me again. Again I just barely heard her say, "Baby, come on back." I went back.

She told me to try once more. I thought she was playing a game. That time I didn't hear her calling, so I looked back. Esty was making funny faces as if talking. I opened the gate and went in.

As soon as I shut the neighbor's gate, Tilly came tearing around the porch, growling and barking. She grabbed my clothes and began shaking me. I hollered and bawled in terror.

The women came out to see what was going on. Mrs. Hentz grabbed Tilly, Mama grabbed me, and we went into the house. Mama looked me over. I didn't have a scratch, and my clothes weren't torn. I was still sobbing a little bit. Tilly was lying there on the floor as though nothing had happened.

Mrs. Hentz said, "I'm sorry that Tilly went after Baby."

Mama was embarrassed about the incident. "It's our fault. I told him to stay home."

When we got up to go home, Mrs. Hentz gave me a piece of licorice candy.

When Mama scolded Esty for letting me come over, Esty defended herself. "I told Baby to come back."

I didn't understand it all and said nothing. Then Esty saw me eating my candy and wondered, "Where's mine?" Her plan had failed; she didn't get candy. She didn't talk much the rest of the day.

I was afraid of Tilly and didn't like her any more. Sometimes I dreamed that she was chasing me. When strange dogs barked, I went into the house. But our gentle collie dog, Fritz, made me feel safe. When I patted him, he reassured me with his friend-ly dog smile. He was my protector.

6

Corn Dale

When we had lived at Amelia about two years, I was three years old. At the edge of the cornfield behind the house was a grove of trees. It shaded a spring producing water that trickled along in a stream among the ferns and moss.

My childhood imagination reveled in the stories Helen told about tiny fairy creatures living in secret hideaways under the ferns. We called the place Corn Dale. It was our private little kingdom.

Helen invented games and played with the little children. Eva thought some of the games were frivolous, but Mama and Papa just laughed.

Helen walked with a limp as a result of the polio she had when she was a little girl. I never noticed it, because she had been that way all my life. The doctor advised us to give her therapy, so every evening we massaged her leg as she lay on the couch. I always took my turn but I didn't know why we did it.

One day while I was laughing and playing rough with Helen, I began to pommel her with my fists. Eva told me, "Stop! You're hurting her."

For the first time, I noticed that Helen limped. I thought it happened because I had hit her so hard. A feeling of guilt plagued me till several years later when I learned the real reason she was lame.

One sunny day when we all should have been working or playing, everyone was subdued and quiet. Mama was sick in bed, and Papa wasn't using jokes to try to cheer her up.

The girls knew the reason, because they were older. A little baby had been stillborn. Papa didn't talk about it, and that made it seem like a mystery to us.

Our little church was composed of only three families, and there wasn't much communication in private matters. We had no minister, and there was no access to a cemetery.

Papa built a little pine casket. He even put three brass hinges on the cover. Eva and Helen wrapped the tiny infant in its little pink blanket and made a soft bed in the little box. In the evening when the children were in the house, Papa went to a quiet spot under a tree at Corn Dale and made its grave there. As if by silent agreement, we didn't play there for a while.

Next to the house was a new field of alfalfa. Papa had strung a wire fence by the road to keep out stray cattle. One day he heard a commotion in the direction of the field. What he saw astounded him!

A motley bunch of mule teams and convicts in striped clothing were going into the field. They had cut the fence and were setting up a work camp in our alfalfa. Papa went to a man who was carrying a shotgun and asked, "What's going on here?"

He said, "We have orders from Richmond to fill and grade the road. We were told to get dirt at the most convenient place, and this is it." He refused to discuss it further; his orders were from Richmond.

Just then Abe Landes, a country storekeeper, came by on his way to Amelia. When he saw what was going on, he offered, "Why don't you let me check up on it in Richmond? I'm going there to do some buying for my store."

On his return, he didn't have much to report: "The highway department will look into it."

A week later, after the field had been ruined, the man with the gun came to the house and left a message for Papa. "We'll be moving on in the morning. I'm sorry about the field. There was some misunderstanding about where we were to get the fill dirt."

Papa made inquiries about compensation, but Richmond never replied. One day when Abe Landes dropped in, Papa stood looking ruefully at his ruined field and commented, "I wonder how often people in authority dismiss their mistakes with nothing but regrets."

Abe sympathized with him. "I think we should pursue the matter further with Richmond."

"Oh, well, I've decided to just let it go as it is," Papa replied.

I was too little to understand any of it, but I could feel the loss and disappointment the family was experiencing. I thought that somewhere there was somebody who ought to be spanked. Then Esty and I went to Corn Dale to watch the little green frogs jump into the water.

7

Building the New House

I knew Papa had built the square house where John Hentzes lived, but I didn't know how he was able to do it. I thought about it sometimes when I was sitting on the floor, building houses with my wooden blocks. But then I began to see how he must have done it.

Papa was building another house down the road toward Promised Land, and he often took me along to get me out of Mama's way. He would hitch up old Farmer to the spring wagon and load up a little hay and some corn for Farmer to eat at noon. Mama would pack a lunch basket for Papa and me. She would include a jar of lemonade or peppermint water.

As we drove along the road, Papa would tell me who lived in the houses by the road. We passed a little country store, then the place where the Halls lived, and down a little further, where the Harvey "girls" lived. We didn't have far to go, so it didn't take long to get there.

As we met people along the way, they would exchange "Hallos" with us. The Harvey ladies would always say, "How y'all doin'?" and Papa would say, "Just fine, thank you."

When Papa said "Howdy" to the men who often worked for us, they always answered the same way: "Tol'ble, tol'ble, thank you." When any of the grown folks said something to me like "Good morning," I didn't know what to say and would just look down toward the ground.

When we arrived at the workplace, Papa would unhitch Farmer and tie him to a post under a tree. Then he would take his tools from the wagon and start working on the house.

I wasn't supposed to go down to the woods. Papa always showed me where to play, usually near a tree where moss and tiny little ferns grew. I liked to watch the ants going around, carrying big hunks of something in their pinchers. But I was afraid of spiders and would chase them away.

It was taking a long time to build the house. Sometimes Papa had two black men to help him. One of them was Branch Purcell, and the other was Shad Bowls. They did work from time to time for us, both at Truehart's and at the new place. Branch always worked without a hat, even on really hot days. So one time Mama bought a straw hat at Staceys and gave it to him. He said "Thank you" to her and went and laid it down beside his lunch bucket.

The next time Branch came to work, he was wearing the straw hat, but it looked different. Under the brim and up into the crown, it was lined with blue cloth. When he saw Mama looking at it, he seemed pleased and explained, "My wife fixed it that way to help keep the sun out a little better and make it fit more nice."

Branch and Shad always worked without shoes. Their feet seemed big and strong. One of Shad's big toes was a lot shorter than the other one. One evening when we asked about it, Papa told us why. "When Shad was a boy, he was working with some older men, cleaning mud out of a ditch. Their bare feet were completely covered by the mud.

"Then, one of Shad's big toes showed just above the mud. He thought it was the head of a snake and whacked it off with the point of his shovel. But now, children, I don't know if this story is true. Just don't ask Shad about it!"

One day after the house was framed way up toward the sky, I sneaked inside to play on the ground inside the house. The two men were not helping that day, and Papa was way up somewhere, nailing on some heavy boards. I was busy playing when, all of a sudden, I heard the sound of a board hitting something.

I looked up just in time to see a plank falling down toward me. I jumped up to get out of the way just as it hit the ground on its end. It stood there for a moment, then it fell over against me real softly and pushed me over. It didn't hurt at all.

Papa came scrambling down really fast and picked me up. He looked me over and asked, "Baby, are you hurt?" He looked quite anxious. I didn't know whether to cry or act brave. I thought it looked as if I was supposed to cry, so I cried—to please Papa. That way he could be nice to me, and it would all seem more important.

He said, "Baby, you know I told you to play out under the tree. I didn't know you were in here."

Eventually the house was all framed up and the rough flooring nailed down. Papa would lead me around sometimes and point out how the rooms were arranged. He helped me up the rough stairs and showed me where our different bedrooms would be. I didn't dare to go inside unless he was with me.

Papa said, "As soon as the chimney is up, I can begin finishing the house inside. The brick man will soon be coming to build the chimney."

Brother asked, "Will we still say we are living at Amelia after we move to the new house near Promised Land?"

Papa said, "Nothing will change much. We will still have the same neighbors and maybe a few more. Our address won't change, because our post office will still be at Amelia."

8

Mr. Maxie

Amelia Courthouse, Amelia County, Virginia—that was our address. We lived in the Truehart's house while Papa was building a new one for us. He often took me along to the construction site. One time after it was all framed up, I was walking along inside with him when I saw, right in front of my face, a shiny object hanging on a string. It was about as big as an egg and pointed at the bottom, with a little hole at the top where the string was fastened.

I started to reach for it, but Papa held my hand and told me not to touch it. I asked what it was, and he said it was a plumb bob. He pointed up through the framing and said, "See, Mr. Maxie is laying the bricks for the chimney and uses the string to help him keep the chimney straight."

When I looked up, I saw, way up there, a man smiling down at me. He was black and had curly gray hair and white teeth.

Papa said, "Mr. Maxie is the mason who is laying the bricks for the house."

I asked Papa, "May I have the plumb bob to play with after Mr. Maxie is done with the bricks"

He laughed and said, "Oh, no, Baby. Mr. Maxie will need it for other jobs."

Finally the house was finished, and we moved in. One Sunday, Papa was sitting in the front room reading, and I was lying on the floor, looking at a picture book. We used the front room only on Sunday or when we had company. Papa looked up from his book, laid it down, and went to the window. He just stood there looking, so I got up and looked out too.

A rectangular black wagon was going past. A black horse pulled it, and a black man was on a seat in the front, holding the lines. I had never seen a wagon like it. It was like a shiny box, with no windows or doors. Several carriages were following it. Everything seemed so black and bleak, and the horses were walking slowly.

I asked, "Papa, what is it?"

"Mr. Maxie died, and that's the funeral."

I didn't understand. "Where's Mr. Maxie? I thought you said he was laying bricks on other jobs."

"Not any more. That big wagon in front is a hearse, and Mr. Maxie's coffin is in there."

I thought about Mr. Maxie and the plumb bob. I wondered about other things but did not know how to ask about them. I remembered what our Sunday school teacher, Annie Weaver, said: "Good people go to heaven when they die." She told us about heaven and Jesus.

I knew what heaven looked like because she showed us pictures. We would sit on the floor, and she would hang a big picture on the wall and talk about it. Sometimes Jesus had children around him, so I knew children were in heaven where Jesus was. Some pictures had sheep and birds, so I knew animals were there, too.

In one scene, Jesus was carrying a little sheep in his arms. Another had a boat on a pond like at Beaver Pond Mill. I understood all these pictures as describing heaven.

One time Annie Weaver told us about a lady who wiped Jesus' feet with the hair of her head. She asked us, "Why do you think the lady did that?"

No one else answered, but I knew, so I replied, "She didn't have any rags to wipe with. Rags are too dirty to have in heaven."

The teacher said, "That's a good thought." She talked about other things I didn't understand. But I did know that good people go to heaven when they die.

We stood watching the carriages going by. I asked Papa, "Was Mr. Maxie good?"

Papa said, "Yes, I think he was good." Then he went back to his chair, picked up his book, and began to read again. I kept watching till the last carriage went by. Then I went back to my picture book on the floor.

I was glad Mr. Maxie was good, I thought he would like it in heaven, and I wondered what had happened to the plumb bob.

9

Mary Ella

I was about four years old when we moved into the new house Papa had built. We called it the Yellow House because the last one we lived in was white. The five children in our family were in two groups—"the girls" and "the children."

The girls were Eva, fifteen, and Helen, thirteen. The children were Esty, Brother, and Baby. I was still Baby and didn't mind being called that. Esty was Esther, six years old. She could read already. Nine-year-old Brother was always making things and drawing. His real name was Benjamin Franklin. Papa called him "Boy!" when he was giving him work to do.

We were the only Pennsylvania Dutch (German) family living in Amelia. We were in Virginia and the South. Our neighbors were friendly, and I noticed that some were black. The black neighbors didn't live along the road but on lanes running back through the fields. Mary Ella's home was across the field from our house.

One day Mama walked across the field and asked, "Could Mary Ella help me in the house?"

An agreement was made. Mary Ella was fourteen, and her speech was somewhat different from the English we knew, but not as different as Pennsylvania Dutch was to her ear. I understood her most of the time.

The first day Mama showed Mary Ella how to set the table, but Mary Ella didn't count right. Mama added another plate and told us to come to the table. Mary Ella just stood by the kitchen door and looked embarrassed.

Mama said, "Come on, Mary Ella, you can sit here by me and Baby." My highchair and I were always an attachment to Mama.

Mary Ella replied, "No'm, Miz Web'. I'ze gwin ter eat in de kitchen," and that's how it was. Mama let her fix her own plate in the kitchen.

One Sunday afternoon Mama called me in from play, washed my hands and face, and put me in clean rompers. I guessed we were going to visit someone. I hoped they would have candy. Papa put me in the buggy, helped Mama get in, and climbed in himself. He took up the lines and drove out the lane.

I persuaded Mama to let me sit on the outside. "I want to watch the wheel roll along the road." I liked to see it make its track in the dirt. I would spot the joint in the rim as it came around and see if I could say, "Twinkle, twinkle, little star," while it made one turn. When Papa made the horse go fast, I couldn't keep up.

We rode along till we came to an opening in a fence by the road. Papa turned the horse in and drove along the edge of a meadow to where a lot of people were standing and sitting around a pond. He got out and tied old Flory, the horse, to a bush.

Papa stretched out the horse blanket under a willow tree, and we sat down on it.

Mama whispered to Papa, "Do you see Mary Ella?"

Papa didn't answer. He never spoke unless he had something to say.

Then Mama exclaimed, "Oh, there she is!" The people were singing, and it sounded so different from our singing in church at Promised Land Schoolhouse. I noticed that all the people were black, so I figured that they sang better than white people.

Soon a big man in a dark suit got up and spoke. The people would say, "Yes, Lawd," and nod. Then two men walked down into the water, waist deep. Another person led a girl into the water till she stood between the two men. One of them said something, and they lowered the girl backward into the water three times. The man who led her in also led her out of the water.

When she came back on the shore, her white dress was all wet. Two ladies took a purple sheet and threw it around her as they sat down. More people went into the water, and then it was Mary Ella's turn. As she returned, wading out of the water, Mary Ella said with a joyful voice, "Glory, I done lost my sins in de wabes."

I knew she meant "waves," but I didn't know what "sins" were. I didn't see anything in the water

but ripples. All the while we were sitting there, a large bright blue bird was making loud noises in the trees nearby. When I tried to get up to look at it, Mama took hold of me and made me sit down.

On the way home, I sat between Papa and Mama. I always felt cozy and safe when I was between them. "Mama," I asked, "what happened to Mary Ella?"

"She was baptized."

"Why?" I asked.

"Ask Papa." But Papa didn't answer. I guess he thought I was too little to understand.

Then I wondered, "What was that big blue bird hollering about?"

Papa said, "That was a blue jay, and I guess it didn't want us too close to its nest."

Mama said something to Papa in Pennsylvania Dutch, and he answered. I felt warm and cozy and squeezed Mama's arm a little because I knew I was important enough for them to talk about in their secret way. After that day, Mary Ella sang a lot. I thought that maybe sometime she would tell me about her dip in the pond, but she didn't.

10

The Heatwole Flower

Lewis James Heatwole was out in our yard, carefully examining the white flowers on the mallow bush Mama had planted by the house. The flowers were as big as saucers and had pink centers. It was a lovely Sunday morning in June.

Bishop Heatwole had arrived in Amelia the day before and was staying at our house. That morning he was going with us to our church at the Promised Land Schoolhouse. He was to be in charge of the communion service.

We were all ready for church, waiting in the yard. Papa was at the barn, hitching the horse to the surrey. Mama and Bishop Heatwole were talking about the flowers.

Mama joked, "Since you like them so much, you'll have to come back again in the fall. I'll dig up some roots for you."

He replied, "I can't come then, but you can just

send some to me at Harrisonburg [Virginia]."

Papa drove up with the surrey. As many as could fit, packed themselves in. It was so full that Brother and I had to stand on the steps, one on each side, holding to the door frames. We enjoyed riding like that and used to beg to do it. The girls never stood on the steps; it wasn't ladylike.

That morning twenty-seven people were at church. The bishop looked just like a prophet, standing there with his white beard and raising his arm to point at imaginary stars. He was telling about the children of Israel and how God said they would be as many as the stars in the sky.

Papa had told us, "L. J. Heatwole knows a lot about the stars and weather."

After church, I wanted to ask Bishop Heatwole something about the stars. I didn't get a chance because he was going to be at Sam Weaver's for the rest of the day. Maybe he would say something more about stars in the evening, when he preached again.

However, L. J. Heatwole didn't mention the stars when he preached that night. Sam Weaver again led a song in which we prayed, "Thy will be done." I thought "Thy" was the name of a little boy who was slow at eating his oatmeal. Sooner or later, "Thy will be done" with his breakfast. I knew how that was, since it was the same way with me.

On the way home after church that night, the moon was full and everything seemed ghostly. I had never been out so late at night in full moon. Even though it was night, I could see cows standing in the field. As we turned in at our place, I saw a rabbit hopping on the road. We stopped by the big gum

tree, and everyone got out. The others started for the house while Papa put the horse away.

Then I remembered that I had left my Sunday school card in the surrey and ran back to get it. I thought the rest would wait for me, but when I turned around, they were going into the house. Papa was in the barn, and I was all by myself—in the moonlit darkness!

There were strange sounds in the bushes, and I was too frightened to move. I was afraid the "Old Frozen Lady" would get me like Esty had said. The Old Frozen Lady was a scary legend among us children. She had been an old lady with a wandering mind and body. She would slip out of the house and go knocking on doors in our neighborhood, calling, "Where is my Mah-ma?"

Our neighbors would always lead her back home. One cold night the old lady was missing, and they found her huddled against an empty house, frozen to death.

Just as I was about to panic, Papa came to the surrey to get his Bible before he went in the house. When he saw me, he exclaimed, "Why, Baby, what are you doing here?"

I just said, "I'm scared." I took hold of his arm, and we started toward the house. Then I noticed a dark, long shape on the ground and asked, "What's that, Papa?"

"Oh, that's just the shadow of the gum tree. The moon couldn't shine through the tree, so it made a shadow. See, we have shadows too."

He showed me our moving shadows, and I felt safe again.

Then I pointed to the mallow bush and observed, "Look, the L. J. Heatwole flowers aren't blooming any more."

Papa explained, "The flowers close at night and open in the morning. They're just like boys. They go to sleep at night."

In the house, the others were all talking and eating sugar cakes. Mama had put a dishful on the table, and Papa and I each took one, too. I said to Mama, "Did you know that the L. J. Heatwole flowers sleep at night?"

She laughed. "Yes, I know that."

Then I turned to Esty and declared boldly, "The Old Frozen Lady didn't get me!"

Eva as big sister had to give her usual friendly correction about such matters. "There are no ghosts, Baby, and you don't need to be afraid of the Old Frozen Lady. She wouldn't have hurt you even when she was alive."

But on dark nights when the wind blew, I was still sure I could hear her calling "Mah-ma" and trying to get in the back door.

11

Charlie Wallace and Lost Honor

Papa liked oatmeal cookies. Mama decided to make a batch of them, but she needed more oatmeal. She said, "Baby, here, take this. Go over the field to Weaver's Store and get some oatmeal. Let them read the note."

As usual, she wrote a note, wrapped it around some coins, and tied it all up in a neat little package. On the way I passed the knee-deep pond Brother had made. Right there in the middle was his pet duck, Charlie Wallace, taking it easy. Eva said it was wrong to name the duck Charlie Wallace. She thought it was making fun of a funny crooked little man we knew with that name, who waddled like a duck when he walked.

As I trotted along on my way home, carrying the

oatmeal, I kept rhythm by saying, "Bomalick, boma-lick, bomalick," to myself. Esty said it was a bad word, but I couldn't get it out of my mind. Several days before she had heard Papa and Mama talking together in Pennsylvania Dutch. That meant they didn't want the children to know what they were saying.

Esty thought she heard Papa say "Bomalick." She asked Mama what "bomalick" meant. When Mama said she didn't know what it meant, Esty was sure it was a word children shouldn't say. Esty told me about it, and we both repeated it several times. Then she told me never to say it because it was "a bad word." Helen and we younger children had worked out a set of rules about things that were bad or good to say. Our notions often gave way before the weightier judgments of Eva.

Passing by the pond on the way home, I saw Charlie Wallace still resting at the same place. I was going to shout, "Hey! Charlie Wallace!" But because of Eva's ruling, I threw a pebble instead. Something was wrong. Charlie didn't move.

When the others came home from school, I told Brother, and we went to see about it. Brother waded in and picked Charlie up. There was only a thin red neck curling out through the feathers where his head had been. A snapping turtle had bitten it off.

Eva said perhaps it had happened as our punish-ment for making fun of the real Charlie Wallace. Helen and Brother didn't think the duck was to blame, so why did he lose his head? I knew why. It was because he was always sticking his head down in the water.

The incident prompted Helen to think of ways she could treat her own little bantam hen with greater care. She decided to feed it at noon as well as in the morning and evening. Since I wasn't going to school yet, she made me to promise to feed it at noon. She put some feed in a broken cup and told me where to put it right after lunch. She said, "Do you promise on your word of honor not to forget?"

I promised. "Word of honor" was a most solemn promise, subject to penalty if not fulfilled. But I did forget.

Helen was disgusted with me. She said, "Baby, you lost your honor."

Once before, in a similar situation, I had earned back my honor by running all kinds of errands for her. So I said, "I'll do something for you, Helen."

She said, "Baby, that won't work this time."

I pleaded, "I want a way to get my honor back."

She worked out a solution: "If you get three different people to jerk your arm three times while you say with each jerk, 'I'm sorry I lost my honor,' it will then be restored."

It seemed almost too easy. Esty was the first one to help and was followed by Brother. But when Helen said that she, as the aggrieved person, couldn't help, I knew I was in trouble. Eva would never, never do such a trivial thing. I could sense in my bones the result if I asked her. But I got up my nerve and tried.

As expected, she said the idea was foolish and then gave me kindly advice about being sorry and trying to do better. But Helen left me crying in remorse for my lost honor.

Helen knew I was sorry, so she told me to stand real straight before her and look right into her eyes. Then she said, "Baby, are you sorry you lost your honor?"

I said, "Yes." She made me say it three times.

Then she said, "Will you try not to do it again?"

I said, "Yes." She made me repeat it three more times.

"Now," she said, "you have your honor back."

I was glad, but I thought maybe she was going to declare that three times, too. Both Eva's and Helen's requirements had been met, and I was happy again.

Doing Things

12

Elements of Self-Expression

Brother was always building something. Down by the pine woods near the pond, he was constructing playhouses. Each of us four younger children were to have one. Eva was above such "child's play."

We dragged down leftover lumber from the new house, and he began to build Helen's playhouse, which turned out to be the biggest. Brother's was a bit smaller, and Esty's was rather small and oblong with only three sides.

Mine was an imaginary house, traced out on smooth ground with its walls represented by a border of fieldstones. An opening in the stones suggested a doorway.

Helen kept her play costumes, consisting of discarded adult clothing, neatly displayed on wall hooks. Brother kept his hammer and saw and a cocoa box full of assorted nails in his playhouse.

I was satisfied with my house, because I was a beneficiary of the same rules that applied to the others. Rule one provided that no one could enter another's house unless invited. That was especially important when being pursued.

A special rule applied to my house. Since its walls were imaginary, we were forbidden to step over the walls to enter. We must always enter by the door. If, when being pursued, I jumped over the walls, the one pursuing could also jump over. Only by entering the door would I be considered to be officially safe.

Helen's house also became a center of the performing arts. Here she had us recite poems, sing songs, and perform plays.

In preparation for a recital, Helen was writing her latest play. She was sure Mama and Papa would enjoy it and that Eva would approve of it. By then, Eva was in high school, and as Miss Percival's favorite student, she would receive extra books to read. Helen had sneaked the copy of *Elements of Self-Expression* that Eva's teacher, Miss Percival, had loaned her for outside reading. She reread the chapter on drama several times. Helen decided that her play would be about the Civil War.

Right around Amelia the last battles of the Civil War had been fought. The army of northern Virginia had been forced to abandon Richmond, burning it as they left. They tried to make a stand at Petersburg but had been outflanked. General Ewell had to surrender his corps to Sheridan at Amelia. The next day, Robert E. Lee had surrendered to Ulysses Grant at Appomattox Court House, about forty miles west of

Amelia, near Lynchburg. So the war was over on May 26, 1865.

That had been just fifty years earlier, and the older folks who had seen it still had deep feelings of defeat. They would say, "If only we could have held on a little longer." But all their supplies had been cut off.

The culture passed down to the young people the romance of heroism and bravery in battle. In school we still sang "Dixie" and "The Bonny Blue Flag." "Uncle" Gholson, the old black man who cleaned up around Amelia High, used to say, "Yes, suh! I dun poh'd coffee fo' Gen'l Lee. Gen'l Lee, he goo-od man." When the children said "Hi, Uncle Gholson," he would touch his hat. But when the teachers said "Howdy," he would lift his hat, bow slightly and say, "Tol'ble, thank ye."

Helen was putting the finishing touches to her play. How could she best use the talents of her cast? Brother was nine years old. Esty was seven, and I was four. It was a challenge, but she felt excitement when she contemplated the results. She even considered charging admission. But most of all, she wondered if Eva would appreciate the subject and the performance.

Helen had completed the play, and the cast had run through a practice performance. Helen thought everyone did well, and she told them so. The book *Elements of Self-Expression* said that a plot should be understandable. She carefully outlined it on her pencil tablet:

PLOT
Mother, whose son has gone to war and who was the hero in a great battle. The battle was won, but the son lost his life. The mother says it was not in vain. But then she learns that, alas, the war was lost! (The book said that sadness must not be expressed without some control and an element of strength.)

CASTING
Brother: A soldier friend and the bearer of news
Esty: Mother, very patriotic (a widow)
Baby (me): Son, a soldier brave and true, off to battle
(All are wearing appropriate costumes.)

The play was performed before a packed house consisting of Mama, Papa, and Eva. They all had paid admission—one penny each.

SCENE I
Mother, dressed in long skirt and dust cap with frills, is sitting before the door. Her son (Baby) stands by her side. They softly sing, "We are a band of brothers, native to the soil. . . ." She is putting the final stitches in the Bonny Blue Flag lying across her lap. She rises and hands the flag to her son. They embrace, and off he goes to war.

SCENE II
Mother, shading her eyes, peers into the distance. A soldier is approaching. He is carrying someone. It is her son! He was killed in battle. The soldier says how bravely her son fought and that the battle was won. He carries her son into the house, bumping the

67

son's head against the door as he goes. (The actor remembers he is "dead" and doesn't say "ouch.")

The soldier hands Mother the flag her son had brought to battle. She holds it aloft and sings in true theatrical fashion, "Oh, why should we lament his loss, when he won for the dear Sunny Southland a banner like this?"

SCENE III

The soldier finally takes courage and explains to the mother that, although the battle was won, the war was lost! The mother breaks down and weeping bitterly, quotes, "Oh, 'tis hard for one to fold it. Hard for one who once unrolled it, now to furl it with a sigh." She holds the flag to her breast.

CURTAIN

Everyone applauded. The play was described as excellent. I was a star. Mama said she was sure I was going to cry when Brother bumped my head. Helen distributed the box receipts equally among the cast. Eva told Helen it was good, but she didn't think we ought to always be talking about the Civil War.

As the others went toward the house, talking as they went, I went to my playhouse. Remembering to enter by the door, I lifted one of the stones and hid my penny underneath.

13

Eva

Expressed in terms of civil government, Papa would have been president, Mama would have been vice president, and Eva would have been secretary of state. The rest of us children were the regular citizens, with Helen in charge of games and recreation.

Eva possessed a certain sophistication that commanded respect. At the age of sixteen, she related maturely to Papa and Mama, while keeping an amiable association with the rest of us. Except for Brother being spanked by Papa from time to time, life was pleasant and enjoyable.

Then one day our tranquility was shattered. Eva was sent home from school, deathly sick with a high fever and in severe pain. As she lay on the couch, I knew something was wrong because she wouldn't talk to me. Mama was putting cold, wet cloths on her forehead, while Papa went to get Dr. Davenport.

The doctor put a thermometer in her mouth and

took out his watch as he held her wrist. He slowly shook his head. Papa and Mama looked worried as he felt around her stomach and asked questions.

Then Dr. Davenport took them into the next room to talk. I went along, but they paid no attention to me. I couldn't understand what they said. Later I learned that Eva had a ruptured appendix and that it was beyond surgery. Peritonitis had set in. Few people survived such a crisis.

Despite the fact that Dr. Davenport said it was useless, Papa made him wire the Richmond hospital and arrange to take Eva there at once by train. I remember Eva being carried out of the house on a stretcher. At the hospital, all they could do was install a tube to drain her body cavity and let nature take its course. Papa stayed with her, and we all were in a state of shock. We could not imagine home without Eva.

Finally, after several days, Papa came home. He said the doctors thought she might make it. She would have to stay in the hospital until her temperature became normal and stayed that way for two days. Everyone was relieved. Miss Percival sent her a get-well card, and we sent drawings and notes with Papa when he went to see her. Then at last, she was well enough to come home.

I was shocked when I saw Eva. I expected to see her marching across the yard with a cheery "Hallo!" But she was brought in on a stretcher and placed on the sofa. She was thin and pale. Her sparkling brown eyes were dull, and her beautiful black hair had been shorn. She looked like a scarecrow.

As spring became summer, Eva's hair grew back

and her health was gradually restored.

One day Dr. Davenport came to talk about "this remarkable case." He talked and talked while Mama was putting a dish of fresh sliced tomatoes on the table. Then he said, "Mrs. Weber, I wonder if I might taste some of those nice tomatoes?"

Mama said, "Sure," and gave him a fork. He began to fork whole slices into his mouth as he continued to talk through drip and spray. I was afraid he would eat them all and said plaintively, "Baby likes them, too!"

When Eva went back to school in the fall, she began a new interest. Mrs. Wooten, the music teacher, encouraged her to practice on the organ during recess. She loaned her a simple book of songs to work on.

Since we had no organ at home, Eva drew a keyboard on a strip of heavy paper and laid it on the sewing machine. There she practiced as she sang, "Lightly row, lightly row, o'er the glassy waves we go." Sometimes she would make a mistake on her imaginary keyboard and say, "Oh, that was wrong!" and start over again. She asked Papa to get an organ, but he was non-committal on the subject.

When Papa had a construction job a distance from home, he would stay there several days at a time. The afternoon of his return, Esty and I would play the windowsill game. We imagined a line on the windowsill as the way Papa would come home. One end was home, and the other end was Amelia.

We placed a button on the line, representing Papa's wagon close to Amelia, and then we moved it bit by bit toward home. We tried to make it come out just right with his arrival. When we finally saw him coming, we quickly adjusted the button to make it work out.

One time Eva came to look out the window where we were playing windowsill. She saw Papa coming with the two-horse wagon. We adjusted the button, and then Eva suddenly said, with delight and laughter, "Look! I believe Papa has an organ on the wagon!"

Sure enough, there was a long square box on the wagon. Eva excitedly began to wonder where we would put the organ. But as the wagon drew close, the big box turned out to be a large mortar box, standing upright on its side.

Eva never did get her organ, and her music career withered. But other things captured her interest. Mr. Outland, the principal, commended her for her public speaking ability. Then, too, Miss Percival was going to take her to Richmond on a personal cultural tour. Eva never practiced "Lightly Row" any more.

14

The "Funny Thing"

Brother was humming excitedly and shuffling his feet as he watched the little waterwheel spin. He had just put his latest invention into operation. Brother called it his "funny thing."

It consisted of an old five-gallon molasses can mounted on a wooden frame. By punching a hole in its side near the bottom, he directed a stream of water against a little paddle wheel mounted in its path. He had worked at it long and patiently, often sneaking time from his work when Papa was away.

I felt a part of the project because I handed him the hammer or held a board while he nailed. We both imagined Papa would look pleased and maybe smile a little when he saw it. Papa seldom gave compliments; he just smiled and looked pleased. We always looked at Papa's face to see how he felt about things.

Once more Brother had filled the can with water from the pond, and the wheel spun merrily. Then our concentration on the "funny thing" was interrupted by the sharp voice of Papa calling, "Boy!"

Brother was scared. Papa wasn't supposed to be home yet, and he wasn't finished with his job. He knew he was in trouble for neglecting his work, since he was already under the promise of "a good dressing-up," as we called it in our family.

Corporal punishment was understood in terms of degree and to some extent in terms of gender. A dressing up was a scolding administered with a bit of corrective switching. A spanking was concerned more with minor misdeeds of the moment.

Paddling was for girls or babies. When Mama paddled Esty, there was always a swirling of skirts. Esty cried like a girl, but I didn't believe it hurt that much. However, when Mama paddled me, it really hurt because I was wearing short pants and didn't have a dress to cushion my legs. I tried to sound loud like Brother when I bawled so Mama would stop sooner.

One form of punishment in those days deserves special note—the thrashing. To us children, it seemed to be a threat against life itself. It was administered with a strap.

Thrashings were the subject of tales and rumors. We heard of a boy who was thrashed until he bled. Then there was the boy who ran away after being thrashed. In one account he never returned. In another version he came back only to be thrashed again for running away.

I always imagined that if I was thrashed, I would

hide behind Promised Land Schoolhouse. They would look for me a long time and be sorry.

As Papa approached, Brother trembled with fear. Papa deliberately took out his pocketknife and cut a substantial switch from a tree nearby. With sober admonition, he bent Brother over his knee and began the dressing-up.

Brother's doleful cries came from deep in his throat. He moaned "yes" or "no" in agonizing response to Papa's dressing–up lecture.

I was mad at Papa. I began to cry, too, and to pelt him with pebbles.

Papa said, "Stop it, Baby, or I'll spank you too."

As Papa left the scene, he laid the switch on a post as a reminder. With convulsive sobs, Brother went back to his work. I imagined how Brother would run away with me and hide in the old mica mine behind Kauffman's.

It wasn't much fun to play with the "funny thing" any more. We never took Papa to see it. Under the circumstances, Brother thought he probably wouldn't smile and look pleased.

15

The Copperhead

It was always exciting to Brother and me when Vernon Lynn came with his buzz saw rig to saw our stove wood. One day Papa and Brother were carrying logs together because Vernon was coming the next morning. We were watching out for snakes because the girls said they had seen a snake "down there this side of the pond." Helen thought it was a copperhead.

Vernon Lynn was handy with machinery. He fixed up a saw rig by mounting a one-cylinder gasoline engine on a spring wagon. He drove it without a horse by running a belt from the engine to a pulley attached to one of the back wheels. There was an idler pulley attached to a wooden lever that allowed him to start and stop by tightening or loosening the belt.

He took the front shafts off his horseless wagon and connected a steering yoke to the front axle. The buzz saw was carried along, ready to be set in place on the job site. The same engine was used to run the saw. Brother always imagined how we could fix up an engine on our own wagon and drive around without horses.

The next morning, Brother and I waited at the lane as the rig came pop-popping down the road from Amelia. The wagon looked funny, moving along without a horse and with Mr. Lynn up front holding onto the steering yoke. As it came closer, Brother held Fritz, our family collie, so he wouldn't get excited and bark.

Setting up was no big task, and we were soon ready to begin. Papa said, "Baby, you stand over there and keep Fritz out of the way." Brother was putting on his grown-up look as he helped the men with the sawing. The screaming buzz saw and the popping engine made so much noise that we had to shout to be heard.

After a while, I saw Fritz stop short and look at something in the grass. It was a snake. Fritz jumped and grabbed it and began to sling it around and worry it. The men came and watched. Papa said it was a copperhead and quickly got the axe to kill it. But just then Fritz let out a yelp. The snake had caught his lip! Papa killed the snake, and they all went back to work. Fritz went and stretched out in the shade.

He just lay there as if he was sleeping. When the sawing was finished, Papa came and looked at the dog. His eyes were half closed, and his mouth was pale. It looked as though he was dying. Papa put an old bag under his head and went and got some milk

to try to feed him, but he wouldn't respond.

Toward evening Fritz revived a little and wobbled slowly up to the barn, stopping to rest every few yards. He laid down at his favorite spot by the barn door.

In the morning Mama and I went to the barn with some special chicken and rice for him to eat. On the way we passed the pigpen where the big old pig stayed. The pen was made of boards and was about three feet high, with a roof over one end. Close by, an old hen was scratching around looking for bugs. Mama said, "I bet that hen is hiding a nest in the barn again."

After we fed the dog, Mama had me crawl around in the barn to see if I could find any eggs. I didn't find any, so we started back to the house. Fritz looked much better.

On the way back, we heard loud squawking coming from the pigpen. Mama exclaimed, "The hen is in the pig pen, and the pig has got her!" She jumped into the pen and began kicking the pig's head and hollering at it. She rescued the hen and threw it out, jumping out after it. The hen didn't run away. It just laid there, squawking and flapping its wings.

Mama looked at the chicken and saw that one of its legs was badly hurt. Right there was the chicken killing block, with the hatchet stuck in the top. Mama took the chicken, put its neck between the two nails, and whacked off its head. She told me to stay and watch it while she went to get some hot water.

Fritz came walking from the barn, and we both stood watching the last struggles of the hen. There was a clean area where she had flopped all the trash away. On the stump, pressed between the nails, its head seemed to be alive. Its eyes were wide open, and it was looking at me.

Mama soon came back with a bucket of hot water and proceeded to pluck and dress the hen. She neatly cut off the broken leg and threw it along with the offal and feathers into the pigpen. "There, you mean old pig. If you like chicken so much, eat that mess."

That evening we had chicken noodle soup. It looked good, but I didn't eat any. I remembered the pitiful squawking and could still see the beady eyes looking at me.

16

Then the Chimney Burned

At breakfast one morning, Mama asked if she could use Flory that day. Mrs. Hurst had asked her to come over in the afternoon. Papa said it would be all right. He would use "the other horse" to drive to Bishops, where he was doing some carpentry. After old Farmer died, a neighbor had loaned us one of his horses. We always called it "the other horse." Mama didn't like to drive it.

On his way to the barn after breakfast, Papa sang a few lines as usual. That morning he was singing:

Oh, the glory gates are ever open wide,
Inviting the world to come,
Oh, the glory gates are ever open wide,
To welcome the weary home.

By the time he was ready to drive away, Mama had his lunch bucket packed, and he was on his way. The other children were out by the road, waiting for the school wagon. Oscar Clark, the driver, was late as usual. When they were gone, I went out to play in the sandbox.

It was a warm spring morning. I could hear Mama through the open windows. She liked to sing around the house. In the morning, her singing often woke me. I turned my attention to my project in the sandbox.

I traced out little roads, making turns and make-believe bridges in the sand. The roads were for my "hurry-up wagon" to travel along. The wagon was a little cast-iron truck with its driver molded fast to the seat. Its wheels really turned, but there was a problem that bothered me. I had to pull it with a cord. It would slip off the road at the turns. I wanted to get rid of the string and push it around instead.

To solve the problem, I set the truck on the ground with its cord stretched out before it. Then I took a big hoe to chop off the string. I missed the string and broke the truck into pieces. I picked up the pieces and showed them to Mama. She said maybe Papa could fix it with wire.

I liked the little truck. Papa said it was a special truck that people used to haul things. When they were in a hurry, it was used instead of a horse and wagon. That was why it was called a "hurry-up wagon." Other children had little tin horses hitched to little tin wagons. My truck was special. I began crying and went around the shed, trying to find wire for Papa. I couldn't find any.

After dinner Mama cleaned me up, and we drove away to see Mrs. Hurst. I didn't know who she was, but that didn't matter. Mama said she was a nice lady and had a little boy. First we turned toward Amelia and then left past where Mary Ella lived. As we were passing by a woods, Mama suddenly pulled to a stop and looked past me to the side of the road.

There lying in the weeds was a man. Mama got out of the buggy and sneaked over to him. She looked closely. His mouth was open, and he seemed to be breathing. She stooped over him a little and sniffed. With a look of disgust, she said, "He's dead drunk!" She got back in the buggy, and we were soon at Hursts.

Mrs. Hurst welcomed us and said little Johnny was taking his nap, so we should talk softly. She handed me a book to look at while they talked.

When I saw the book, I knew who she was. The book belonged to a little boy who sat close to us at church. When he sat down on the bench, his legs stuck straight out. Mine hung over the edge, and I could swing them. He would have the book on his lap, and sometimes his mama would open her handbag and give him a mint. Mama never gave me candy in church.

The women talked awhile. They didn't know who the man beside the road might be. Then little Johnny woke and came in the room. When he saw me with his book, he grabbed it and clutched it close. His mama said that wasn't nice, but he wouldn't give it up.

On the way home, we looked for the man, but he

was gone. I asked Mama how a man that was dead could get up. She laughed and said that he wasn't really dead. When someone drank too much whiskey, he fell fast asleep for awhile. It was often called being "dead drunk."

At supper that evening, Mama told about the man. Papa said he had an idea who it could have been, but we shouldn't talk about it. While we were still at the table, I brought Papa the broken truck. He looked at it and said he might be able to patch it with wire.

The next morning, I could hear Mama singing down in the kitchen. I could smell pancakes and cocoa. I felt good because we were having my favorite breakfast, and Mama was singing my favorite song:

There is a happy land, far, far away,
Where saints in glory stand, bright, bright as day,
Oh, how they sweetly sing, praises to their Savior King,
Long may their praises ring, praise, praise for aye.

I was big enough to dress myself and was soon down with all the rest. It was Saturday.

Mama was doing her Saturday baking, and it would take most of the day. All of us were busy doing something.

Then late in the afternoon, Brother came running and shouting, "The chimney's burning; the chimney's on fire!" In no time all of us were running around, talking and hollering.

Esty and I were bawling. My parents and sisters and brother remembered how their house had burned years ago. The second time the flames roared out of the chimney. Mama was dragging a ladder from the barn.

Then Papa took charge. He raised his voice and said, "Stop and listen! The house won't burn. The chimney is good and tight." He told Mama, "Close the stove damper to cut the draft."

Eva and Brother filled several buckets with water. Sparks might start a fire on the ground. Just to play it safe, he set the ladder against the house.

Finally the fire burned out. Nothing bad happened. Papa explained, "We burned a lot of pine, and the chimney hasn't been cleaned yet this year."

At supper Mama set out some sugar cookies she had baked. She tried to make a little joke: "These cakes are partly to be blamed for the fire."

It seemed funny, but I was still scared. It was hard to laugh.

17

Flory's New Shoes

We had a horse named Flory. She was a friendly sorrel, and I liked to reach up and pat the side of her face.

Our family had owned two other horses. Eva was old enough to remember Topsy and talked about her. Papa had sold her to a cousin before we moved to Virginia. There was also a black horse named Farmer. He was Papa's buggy horse, way back before he married Mama. By last summer, Farmer couldn't work any more, and the girls would lead him down to the pond to drink.

One afternoon on the way back from the pond, Farmer stumbled and fell. When he couldn't stand up again, Eva went to get Papa. Papa looked at him and slowly shook his head.

By that time, Mama and the rest of the family had gathered around, stroking old Farmer and encouraging him. Papa said, "Maybe after resting overnight,

Farmer can get up again." Then we all went to the house for supper.

In the morning, Papa reported, "Old Farmer is dead. When horses get really old, they often fall for the last time and never get up again. Some people try to lift them, but it doesn't help."

Later I heard Papa telling Eva in the next room, "Often when a horse is down for the last time, he is shot to put him out of his misery."

I wondered if that was what had happened to old Farmer. No more was said about it. We all cried when they took Flory and dragged old Farmer far away into the woods.

That had all happened last summer. Now Papa was saying, "I need to get Flory's shoes fixed."

I tried to understand how a horse got shoes. Brother said, "The blacksmith will cut off some of the feet and then nail on the shoes." I imagined the blacksmith would take a big knife and cut off her feet and somehow fasten on some new ones. I couldn't bear to think about how much it would hurt Flory.

So when Papa wanted to take me along to the blacksmith, I wouldn't go. He was surprised because I usually was glad to go along anywhere. Papa questioned me, but I wouldn't tell why. When he came back with Flory trotting along and pulling the buggy, I guessed it had come out all right. But I didn't look at her feet till the next day.

Then I heard Mama say, "It's a good thing Flory had her shoes fixed before she has to pull the spring wagon all the way to Beaver Pond Mill." Papa went to the mill to get feed for the cow. Mama said, "I want to get some of our corn ground for cornmeal."

I didn't like cornmeal mush, but I did like fried mush with butter and molasses.

Mama claimed, "Our ground cornmeal is better than what we get at Stacy's Store."

Papa laughed. "Maybe Stacy's get their cornmeal at Beaver Pond Mill, too."

Mama insisted, "I can tell the difference."

Since we would be going to the mill tomorrow, we had to shell the corn today. Mama had a tub full of ears ready that she had dried in the oven. Papa grabbed the tub in both hands and told me to come along and help.

We went to the barn, and Papa set the tub down by the corn sheller. He stationed me next to the tub and showed me how to stick an ear of corn into the sheller. When he turned the crank, the kernels dropped into a bucket. He would take the cob and throw it on the cob pile. By the time the tub was empty, the bucket was almost full of grain.

Papa set the empty tub and the bucket of corn out in the yard. He said, "We'll have to winnow the corn."

I didn't know what that meant. It sounded like some kind of punishment. However, all he did was slowly pour handfuls of corn into the tub. There was a breeze, and I could see bits of corncob trash blowing away.

Papa said, "Winnowing is a way to blow trash out of things." He put some grains of corn in his hand and mixed some dirt with them. Then he wiggled his hand and blew the dirt away. The corn was clean. I had learned something new.

At supper he told Mama, "Baby really helped me get the corn ready. He even held the bag open while I was pouring in the shelled corn."

Mama asked me, "Are you going along with Papa to the mill, Baby? If so, I'll pack some lunch for you too."

"Yes, I want to go along," I replied.

I had to go to bed early because we would be leaving first thing in the morning.

After an early breakfast, we were on our way. Flory had no problem pulling the wagon, so I knew her feet didn't hurt anymore. We went on a road through some swampy woods. Poles were laid across it like a washboard so the wagon wouldn't sink in the mud.

While we drove through the swamp on that corduroy road, I put my hands over my face so the "infantile paralysis fly" wouldn't bite me. Somewhere I had gotten the idea that such a fly had bitten Helen and had made her sick.

We finally got to Beaver Pond Mill, and Papa tied up at the post. When he finished telling the man what he wanted, he took me out to the pond. Since it would take awhile to grind the meal, we got in a boat and rowed around in the pond. He pointed out some water birds and bushes that we didn't have at home.

Papa had brought our lunch basket with us in the boat. We each had a jelly sandwich and a sugar cookie. Mama also had included a little dish of cornstarch pudding for each and some lemonade.

When everything was ready and loaded up, we started home. I was happy. The boat ride had been fun, and I felt important. I had helped with the work and had learned about winnowing. I was as good as Esty and almost as good as Brother. I never compared myself with Helen and Eva. I just tried to please them.

Then I finally got up the nerve to ask Papa about Flory's feet. "How did they sew her feet on again?"

"Why, what do you mean?"

"Flory's new horseshoes."

Papa laughed and told me, "It's just like when Mama cuts your fingernails. It doesn't hurt." After he explained some more, I was satisfied. But it did hurt when Mama cut my fingernails—she squeezed my hands so hard to keep me from moving.

As we bumped across the poles on the way home, I was happy. I didn't even think about the awful flies. Sometimes Papa seemed like a big brother.

School and Possums

18

Mishoos

"See the cat." That's what Miss Hughes said the words were in my schoolbook. It was easy, because right there was a picture of the cat. Miss Hughes was gentle and caring and did not scold me. She gave me a first-grade reader and treated me like a scholar.

I had been in school three weeks and still couldn't read. I looked across the room to the second-grade section, where Esty sat next to Ruth Lush. Ruth was raising her hand and waving it slightly to attract Miss Hughes.

Ruth pointed the index finger of her other hand to a word in her book. She pressed her finger against the book so hard that its joints made a double curve. I always watched the second grade, so I would know how to act when I was a second-grader.

School failed to come up to my expectations. I assumed that by going to school, I would somehow begin to read. But I was only four and a half, too young for first grade. It was more like preschool for me, or kindergarten, though we did not use that term. Yet the experience helped to train me for later school life.

Recess time was pretty good—until one day Esty spoiled it. During recess, I would always hang around, watching her play with her friends the same as I would have at home.

She used to come to me and whisper, "Go and play with the boys."

Then one day, when I got all excited with what they were playing, I grabbed Ruth by her arm and hugged it. Ruth giggled in embarrassment.

"Baby! Go on away," Esty scolded.

I was mortified. At school I learned that I was supposed to be Levi, a real boy, not "Baby." The result was instant and conclusive. I began to play with the boys.

Around home, Esty was always talking about "Mishoos." That's how she pronounced "Miss Hughes." So that's what I thought her name was. I always called her Mishoos. I liked her because sometimes she helped me with my coat. One time she held my hand to help me copy a "k" from the ABCs on the blackboard.

Another time, when no one was close, she said to me softly, "Levi, my name is Miss Hughes." She said it again, slow and distinctly. Then she got me to say it back to her. She said, "Thank you," and patted my shoulder. It was a special experience. I cherished it as a secret and decided not to mention it to Esty.

I thought Miss Hughes was the nicest and prettiest person I knew. She had blue eyes and soft brown hair. The little white handkerchief she carried smelled like violets.

One day at noon recess, Esty and I walked up the boardwalk along the dirt street. We headed for the stores because each of us had two pennies. We were going to get candy at Stacy's. On the way back, we walked in the road because two teachers were coming up the walk. They were Miss Hughes and Miss Wingo, Brother's teacher.

Just then an older boy came riding his bicycle on the walk toward them. As he approached them, he turned off onto the road, at the same time tipping his cap to the ladies like a true gentleman would in those years. But the maneuver was too complicated. The bicycle fell over, and he sprawled on the road.

The teachers gave a sympathetic exclamation and went to help him. Miss Wingo recovered his cap, and Miss Hughes dusted him off. Envy and jealousy rose within me! I wished *I* had been the one on the bicycle.

That night in bed, I thought about possible ways and situations in which Miss Hughes could be nice to me. *Maybe sometime I'll stumble and fall near her*, I thought. Then in flights of fancy, I imagined her asking me to carry a big pile of books. I could hear her say, "Why, Levi, how strong you are!"

That night I decided to tell Esty about how Miss Hughes told me to say her name. I would tell her how to pronounce it just right. That would get even with her for calling me "Baby" in front of Ruth Lush. I would tell her about it first thing in the morning. *Second-graders don't know everything!*

19

Mama's Trip

Mama was singing in the kitchen. School was out, and the girls were helping around the house. Eva saw the mailman slow his buggy and drop some mail in our box. She got it and brought it to Mama.

There was a letter to Mama from Granny. When she opened the envelope and unfolded the letter, a check fell out on the floor. Picking it up, she went to the next room to read what Granny had to say.

The next day, after she had talked to Papa, we learned what the letter was about. Granny had written, "It's time for you to come home once, to see me and your *Freindschaft* (relatives). I'm sending a check so there will be no backing out this time."

We also learned that Mama would be going up to Pennsylvania to visit for "about a week or ten days." She would have to go at once while the girls were at home to help. I would go along because the others said I was just in the way at home.

Mama sent letters to Granny and Uncle Sam to say when we were coming. The trip was planned, tickets were in hand, and we were all at the Amelia train station, ready to board. After a lot of "good-byes," we were on the way.

The train took us to Richmond, where we switched to a train for Denbigh. There we stayed overnight at the home of some friends. They drove us to Old Point, where we took a ship to Baltimore. There we boarded a train to Lancaster, Pennsylvania. Often on the trip, Mama told me, "Hurry, hurry." Uniformed men helped Mama with her two big suitcases. I had to run to keep up.

At Lancaster a man Mama knew was waiting for us, with a horse and carriage. His name was Wes Miller. He drove a bread wagon two days a week and was available for carriage driving on off days. Wes lived with his wife, Christy, in a little house at Farmersville. There we were going to visit Uncle Sam and Aunt Sadie Burkholder.

As we drove along, their conversation was in Pennsylvania Dutch. He looked down at me sitting there between them and said, "*Du bisht ein Virginny bu, gell* (you're a Virginia boy, not so)?"

Mama said I didn't understand the Dutch (but I did). So he began to talk in English with some German mixed in. He asked Mama, "Did you hear that a German submarine has been seen off shore near Virginia. The Lancaster newspaper said so."

Mama replied, "Oh, it might have sunk our ship on our way coming here."

We arrived at Uncle Sam's at suppertime. Before we arrived, Mama told me that Sam was my uncle on her side of the family. She wanted to tell me on which side of the family our various uncles and aunts were. When we drove in the lane, they all came out to welcome us. The children were Willy (called Sam's Willy), Ada Mae, and Elmira. Aunt Sadie said supper was on, so we all went in and filled the table.

The next morning Aunt Sadie and Mama went around with the children and me, showing us the place. Mama talked to me as if I was one of the big children. She pointed to a big oak tree standing by itself, on a hill behind the house. Mama said, "That tree is why the home was called Oakalone. We used to live there long ago before you were born. One of Papa's older brothers built the house."

We went to the edge of the road, and she pointed down the road toward a schoolhouse. "That's Fairmount School, where Eva started first grade."

I remembered Eva talking about that school. She had told me that Grandpa Weber was living at Oakalone with my family before I was born.

Just then a funny automobile thing drove into the lane. It had big wheels, looked like a spring wagon, and had two seats. A man and a boy were on the front seat, and two boys were on the back seat.

Mama said, "Oh, that's Uncle Jake and the boys." She added quietly to me, "They're on Papa's side." We went out and Mama greeted them. "Why, hello Jake. Where's Aunt Annie?"

Jake responded, "We're just driving through and stopped in to say hello. Annie's busy at home." He turned around to the boys and said, "Now don't jump out; we don't have time." After talking a little while, the automobile engine began making a noise. The horseless carriage just backed out the lane all by itself and began carrying them up the road toward Brownstown.

I was glad we stayed there another day. All my relatives were nice to me. I guess Wes Miller liked me, too, because he asked Mama, "May I take Levi along on the bread wagon today?"

Mama said I could go.

The wagon was a big box-shaped market wagon. Its roof extended over the front seat. Right behind the seat, a slide door opened to shelves filled with fresh bread and cakes. As we drove along, he would stop at the houses and pull a string to ring a bell. The lady would come out and say what she wanted.

Sliding the door open, he would give her bread or cakes and drop her coins into a slot box. He would always point to me and say, "*Des is ein Virginny bu* (this is a Virginia boy)." Then he would explain who my mama was. But he never gave me one of the cookies.

The next day Wes drove us to Millway, where Aunt Alice and Uncle Amos Huber lived. They were on Mama's side. Granny lived with them.

I asked, "Is Granny on your side, too?"

Mama laughed and said, "Of course. She's my mama."

I never knew that before. I had thought Granny was just Granny.

We stayed there several days. Granny and Mama talked and talked while Aunt Alice joined in as she worked. There was someone they knew who lived at Bird-in-Hand. Aunt Lizzie Gibble lived at

Brunnerville. She was Granny's sister and was on Mama's side. The lady at Bird-in-Hand was not on either side.

I was confused and stopped asking about sides. We always picked sides when we played games. I didn't know what these sides meant. Talk continued about people at Halfville, Stumptown, and Muddy Creek.

Next we went to the big city of Reading, where Uncle Israel and Aunt Mary Weber lived. While we were there, Uncle Dave and Aunt Gertie stopped in to say "hello." Uncle Israel lived in a big house in the city. Their house and furniture were really nice, and the tablecloth and dishes were special. We even had bananas to eat, the first time I had ever tasted them.

I slept all by myself in a big upstairs bedroom, in a great big bed. Mama put me to bed like she did at home. She sat on a chair, and I knelt by her lap and prayed, "Now I lay me down to sleep. . . ."

In the morning when Mama came to get me up, she discovered that I had wet the bed! She apologized to Aunt Mary, who said, "That's all right. If I had a little boy, he would have done it too, sometimes. Our wash girl will take care of it."

The next day it was time to go home. Mama and Uncle Israel said, "Because of the submarines, you ought to go home by train." He helped her change the tickets. Mama got all our things together and packed the suitcases. Uncle Israel and Aunt Mary saw us off at the station.

The trip home was hard. We had to change trains three or four times. We just sat there on our seats, sleeping a lot of the time. At last, after what seemed a long time, we came to Amelia. When the conductor called, "Amelia Station," Mama exclaimed, "Oh, joy!" It was night, and all I remember is going to bed.

I dreamed I was getting on a train when the door slammed. It started off, leaving me standing on the step and holding onto the handrail. Gaining speed, it swung around a curve with such force that the handrail broke loose. I went flying through the air and landed on the roof of Weaver's store.

Then I awoke, safe in my own bed. I was home again.

20

About Possums

At breakfast we all kept on talking about Mama's trip. Finally Papa said, "That's enough. We can talk about it again in the evening." He went out, hitched up Flory to the spring wagon, and drove to Amelia. Papa took his lunch along because it was too far away to come home at noon.

Brother and I walked down to the barn. We had cleanup work to do.

I could tell Brother had something on his mind because he was humming quietly as we worked. He finally said, "Papa told me about possums. One day when I was talking to Mary Ella Stokes's brother Buck, he told me his papa used to hunt possums in our woods before we moved here.

"Every year at Thanksgiving time, he would go at night and shoot one or two. Buck said, 'Possums sho am good eatin'.' Our papa said they could hunt there again if they wanted to."

Then Brother went on telling a whole bunch of stuff Papa had said about possums and possum hunting.

Possums were a special kind of animal. They slept in the day and went snooping around at night. They had eyes that could see in the dark. They could hang by their tails from tree limbs and sleep upside down.

When baby possums were born, they were as little as kidney beans. The mama kept them in a pouch outside her stomach until they were big enough to crawl. Then they would hang onto her back while they grew enough to take care of themselves. Possums were hunted in the winter when the little ones were all grown up.

We talked more than we worked. I wished I could have been home to hear about the possums. Brother began to talk some more when we heard Mama call for dinner.

On the way to the house, Brother said Papa had shown him a picture of a possum in the big dictionary that was in the front room, where we kept our books. Before going into the house, we washed our hands at the pump and dried them on the towel.

The girls and Mama talked about the cousins and women Mama had met. They asked about what people had for dinner and how the children behaved. Brother and I had nothing to say. We knew they wouldn't be interested in possums.

After dinner Brother and I went into the front room to look at the dictionary. Our hands were still clean so we didn't have to wash them again. It was a rule that no one could look at the books with dirty hands. Brother took the dictionary from the shelf, and we laid on the floor to look for the right page. When we found it, there was a picture of the possum, with its pointed nose and funny tail like a rope.

We tried to sneak out for fear Mama would want to give us some work to do. She saw us and said, "Brother, fill the water bucket."

His regular job was to fill the water bucket and empty the slop bucket. Brother took the bucket from its stand by the wall, where the water dipper hung on a hook close by. He went to the pump and emptied out the leftover water. Then he put in two pumps of fresh water, whirled it around, and emptied it out just to be sure it was clean. Mama always washed the water dipper along with the dishes to make sure it was clean.

We always had to "be sure" about everything: "Be sure you don't forget. Be sure to lock the door." When we were going upstairs to bed, Mama often said, "Be sure to say your prayers." Brother filled the bucket and set it on the stand, and we went down to finish our work at the barn.

We finished and went down to the woods, looking for possums hanging from trees. We started in the woods above the pond, where we found mostly oak and gum trees. No possum. We went to the woods below the pond where the pine trees grew. Still no possum.

Finally, we saw Papa up at the barn, putting the horse in the stable. Going up, we went along with him to the house. When we opened the door, there was the sweet smell of freshly baked sugar cookies in the air. Mama often baked a big batch when she was excited about something. Then, in the evening when everything had quieted down, we would sit around talking and eating sugar cookies.

It was going to be a real sugar-cookie evening. The discussion about relatives continued and gradually changed to names and places.

Eva asked about Fairmount School and Oakalone, where she had lived as a little girl. Papa asked about Uncle Israel, Uncle Dave, and Uncle Jake. I told about Uncle Jake's funny automobile and the banana I had eaten at Uncle Israel's place. I was glad Mama didn't tell how I had wet the bed. I also told about riding with Wes Miller in his bread wagon.

Then for some reason, we began talking about the names of towns and places. I guess it was because Eva was always talking about Oakalone. Helen thought it was such a romantic name. Everyone began asking about some of the funny names: Bird-in-Hand, Stumptown, Halfville (was it a half town, ha, ha?).

Papa even got in the game. He said there was a little village where all the houses had picket fences. The people called it "Klapboard Shtettle (picket-fence village)." Brother chimed in about Beaver Pond Mill. Eva reminded us that Preacher Good came from Wolftrap, Virginia.

Helen asked, "Why don't we make a name for our place here like they did at Oakalone?" We were all in a sugar-cookie mood. Some suggestions were "Gum Tree Place" and "Crooked Lane," since our lane had a bend.

Franklin tried to work in "Possum." Maybe the

pond could be part of the name. Then Eva mentioned the story about a funny schoolteacher who lived at a place called Sleepy Hollow.

Papa broke into a smile and said, "That's it—'Possum Hollow.' " Because Papa said it, no one objected. We tried to see how it would fit. Then Papa admitted, "But our place couldn't have a name like that. Sleepy Hollow was a place where there were hills and hollows. Amelia is low and level."

The name never quite went away. We didn't try to name our place anything. Every now and then, Papa would say to Brother, "All right, let's get things straightened out here at Possum Hollow." He was just kidding. Maybe somewhere in the South there was a place with that name.

21

The Echo

I was standing at the right place near the pond, facing Weaver's Store and their house. We had discovered that if we stood there and shouted "Hello!" the house would answer back to us. But then I couldn't make it answer.

One time Brother hollered, "Shut up!" to it, and it answered, "Shut up!" I thought it sounded mad, but Brother just laughed. I tried one more time, but it would not answer. I thought maybe it was because the Weavers had moved away and the house was empty.

Their oldest son, Willy, had married Clara Kauffman and left. Not long after that the rest of the family also moved away. I was sorry, because Annie Weaver was my Sunday school teacher, and I liked her. She would sing, "Jesus Loves Me, This I Know" in a nice soft voice, and we would try to sing along.

Sam Weaver had led the congregational hymns,

but now just anybody started the songs from where he sat. Teddy, their ten year-old son, was a hero of mine. Once he was real sick with blood poisoning, and he had to eat his dinner in bed. He didn't have to work either for a long time. I tried eating crackers in bed once, but I got crumbs all through the covers.

One day after they had moved, I went with Papa to look at the empty store. Paper boxes and trash were all over the floor. While I was kicking things around, I found a brand-new pocketknife on the floor. I asked Papa if I could have it, but he made me put it right back where I had found it.

Soon after the Weavers left, the Kauffmans also left. They had a small family business, raising and canning tomatoes. Next to their house was a canning factory where the whole family worked. Their family consisted of Eli; his wife, Amanda; and four boys, Ben, Orie, Jess, and Mervin, all at home. Amanda told Mama that the whole family was tired of tomatoes and that they were going to move down to Denbigh.

Mama and I went to say good-bye to Amanda just before they left. I stayed out in the backyard and fooled around at the old sandpile where Mervin used to play when he was little. Weeds had overgrown everything, and the only toys left were two old wooden spools. I wanted to take them home with me, but Mama made me put them right back where I had gotten them.

All of our regular friends whom we knew had moved away, and it was getting lonesome. I missed going to Weaver's Store for odds and ends. We all missed seeing old Eli driving past, sitting in his two-wheeled gig like Humpty Dumpty, with his chin on his chest, snoozing his way to Amelia. We didn't have enough people left to keep the church going, so we just stayed around the house on Sundays.

One Sunday, Mama got us younger ones ready and drove us to the Methodist Church near Amelia. Everything seemed strange to us. The people sat in family groups, and they didn't have someone stand up front to lead the songs. A lady sat at an organ near the front, and when she played, the people just started singing. They all sang the tune together, just like the women. The men didn't sing bass, and none of the ladies sang alto like Clara Kauffman had done at our church.

A little girl sitting right in front of us kept turning around and staring at us. Even while she was singing, which she did quite loudly, she would turn around and look. They were singing "Loyalty to Christ," and during the chorus, she would open her mouth, showing gaps from missing teeth, and sing right into our faces. I was glad Mama didn't take us back again the next Sunday. We just stayed home.

At supper one evening, Papa said, "Maybe we ought to move back to Pennsylvania again."

Mama was overjoyed. She had been homesick from the first day we had left years before.

However, Eva and Helen didn't like the idea. "We have friends here, and we like the school and our teachers."

Esty said, "I'm scared to live up there in Pennsylvania. I've heard that there are a lot of sink-holes in the fields. If we live there, I'll never go out-doors."

Brother commented, "That would be a great adventure, moving to Pennsylvania. I'll look forward to that."

For me, it was quite acceptable to move. Mama had taken me with her to visit in Pennsylvania among relatives. I liked the people and hoped they would keep on giving me cookies when we lived there.

Sometime after that, I was walking around the playhouses Brother had built and wondering what would happen to them after we were gone. I wondered whether anyone would discover our secret hiding places.

I was standing by the pond, wondering about the echo and whether there were any echoes in Pennsylvania. Then I tried again to make Weaver's house talk back. I yelled, "Hello!" That time it answered, "Hello!" right back. I tried several other words, and it sent them right back. Then I got up my nerve and shouted, "Shut up!" The echo sounded real mad, saying "Shut up!" to me just like it had for Brother.

Then I heard someone behind me. It was Esty. As usual, she began making fun of me. But when I told her to talk to the house, she refused. I think she was afraid that it wouldn't answer her, and then I could make fun of her.

22

Mary Elizabeth

After Papa had talked about moving from Amelia back to Pennsylvania, there was a lot of excitement and discussion. However, life soon settled down to normal work and busy school days.

We were driven to school in a covered rig labeled SCHOOL WAGON and drawn by two floppy-eared mules. We entered the wagon by a large back step and sat on two long benches on either side, facing each other.

Oscar Clark, the driver, sat up front on a stool. He laughed and joked with the children and often played simple games. Sometimes he stopped the wagon to play a card game of "Guess the Number" with the older children. He always won. When that made us late for school, we simply said that the wagon wasn't on time.

Since at five and a half years old, I was still a "kindergartner" and not really in first grade, nothing was expected of me. I just enjoyed the whole scene.

Sometimes close to Christmas, Granny would write from her home at Millway, Pennsylvania, and send Mama a check to "get something for the children." Mama would sit down with the Sears Roebuck catalog and make up an order. There was something for everyone.

That year when the Sears Roebuck order arrived, it included a big box of graham crackers and a tin box of peppermint candy. One of my gifts was a cute little rag doll, "Overall Boy," just like the one in the *Overall Boys* book. It had a little blue cap fastened to its head, and its clothes were sewed fast. I named it John Will, but Mama said, "Oh, no, you ought to call it Freddy; it's only a little boy." So I averaged it out by calling it John Will one day and Freddy the next. In the end, Freddy won out.

One Saturday soon after Christmas, a strange man came to see Papa. They walked around the place a while and then came indoors. Mama showed him around the house and asked him to sit down for a cup of coffee. He sniffled and sneezed as they talked, covering his face with a large white handkerchief. He would always say real politely, "Excuse me, Mrs. Weber. I seem to be catching a cold."

After he left and Papa had gone out to the barn, Mama told me without my even asking, "That was Mr. French. I hope he's going to buy our place." Now the talk of moving to Pennsylvania began all over again.

Not long afterward, when we came home from school, Mama wasn't there. Eva said that Papa and

Mama had gone to Richmond but would be back tomorrow. Eva took charge of supper and bedtime in her usual proficient manner. Papa did come back the next day, but Mama wasn't along.

Esty asked about it, with a look of apprehension on her face. Papa just said, "Mama will be back soon."

Then one evening, he said, "I'm going to bring Mama back home tomorrow. She'll be bringing a little baby girl with her."

I could visualize it: Papa and Mama leading a smiling little girl between them.

When they came back, I guessed that they changed their minds about the little girl, because all Mama had was a blanket rolled up in her arms. But Mama came in, sat down in a chair, and pushed the blanket apart. There was the prettiest little black-haired, doll-faced baby I ever saw.

Mama smiled. "This is Mary Elizabeth."

I wondered if she could talk and how soon she would want my toys. The next Sunday, Marie Horst came to see the baby. Mr. Horst told me, "Now you aren't the baby any more."

I just said, "No, now we have two babies." I didn't care much about it. I wasn't using my high chair any more, and I was going to school. Then, too, I began to feel a bit like a big brother.

Soon afterward, we got some news that gave us mixed feelings. Mr. French was going to buy our place! Papa was going on a trip to Pennsylvania to find a place for us to live.

Pennsylvania,
Here We Come!

23

Going Home Again

Mama said, "Well, at last we're going home. I can hardly believe it." She had never felt at home during the seven years we lived at Amelia. At last we were actually on the train, bound for Lititz, Pennsylvania, where she grew up. It was 1917.

For better control on the trip, we were organized in two groups. Eva and Helen kept Esty and Brother in tow, while I hung in with Mama and little six-week-old Mary Elizabeth (Betty).

In Richmond we changed trains for Lancaster, Pennsylvania, and we were running late. Mama had just hustled us into the depot when the stationmaster's voice rang out, "Baal-ti-moor—Laan-caaster—and—Haaver-dee-graas, Gate Number Ten."

"Hurry up, children. That's our train," Mama urged. "We just made it." When we had settled in our seats and were still puffing, Mama commented, "That was close. I wish Papa were along. It would have been a mess if we had missed our train."

Papa was coming on the freight train with our belongings. He had explained how the trip was arranged and about the place to which we were moving. We would be living on a farm and would be farmers. That didn't appeal to me.

He expanded further and said to Brother, "Boy, the playing is over; you are going to be working." Brother was eleven years old. Papa gave us a little lecture about farming, and believe it or not, we began to accept the whole thing as an exciting adventure.

The train moved along smoothly, slowing down at one point for a hairpin turn. Looking out the window, we could see the engine passing us, going the opposite direction. Mama said it again, "I'm sure glad we didn't miss the train."

People were always talking about missing trains. I was afraid every time I got on a train or automobile that it would start before I got on. With horses, it was easy. When everyone was ready, someone just said "Giddap" or slapped the lines, and that was it. With trains and automobiles, I never knew. One time I saw an automobile start away with a lady standing on the road and waving at it. She didn't get on before it started.

We finally arrived at Lititz with no problems. The girls would be staying in a rooming house in Lititz, and Brother and I would be staying at Aunt Alice's with Mama and the baby. The day Papa arrived, we would all get together at the farm. Papa had engaged Mr. Bushong, at the mill nearby, to gather some wagons and haul our freight from the station.

Everything worked out as planned. Friends and relatives came to help. The high point for me was when they unloaded our guernsey cow, Yeloozer, and our family horse, Flory.

Everybody was in a talking mood. One lady told Mama, "Well, Mary, I guess you're glad to be back in America again."

When I introduced Aunt Alice's boy to the girls as "Aunt Melvin," I didn't know why everyone laughed.

Esty was eager to tell me about the boarding house. "They have indoor plumbing, and there is a chain hanging from a tank near the ceiling. When you are finished using this fixture, you just pull the chain, and there is a great noise of running water. But I don't think our farmhouse will have a setup like that."

By the time everything was unloaded, the people went home, and it was getting dark. Everything was strange. It seemed lonesome and empty. I went with Papa and Brother to the barn to check on the animals. There were pigeons making noises in the loft, and mice were squeaking in the trash. A big black cat jumped out of the shadows and ran away. We left the barn and returned to the house.

The house was a big brick two-story building with a front porch. The entrance hall was big enough to have a long open stairway and a fireplace both downstairs and upstairs. Mama had lit some lamps. She took Brother and me to the upstairs bedroom we would share. We were both scared. As we pulled the covers over our heads, I felt some security in having my big brother near. We seemed to have a lot in common now that I was a little older. Earlier I was only his daytime little brother.

As the others moved about the big house, there were echoes, and it seemed as though they came from places that were empty. Strange sounds came from the attic, and chimney swifts were squeaking and fluttering in the fireplace chimneys.

Then just as we were about asleep, a screech owl began its eerie cry outside the window. I finally fell asleep, dreaming strange dreams. A ghost was trying to ride on the back of old Flory.

24

Some Days Are Like That

It was Monday morning, and Esty and I were walking to school. Our route took us out the lane, left on the road, then one and a half miles to Rothsville School, in the village of Rothsville. We had just moved from Amelia, Virginia, and were finishing the three remaining months of the school year. A two-story brick building served all classes from grade one through high school.

The front entrance reminded me of a big ugly face. Its wide concrete steps, ten of them, led up to a large open foyer that was like a huge maw, swallowing the children streaming through it when the morning bell rang. I was six and didn't like the school. Miss Null, my first-grade teacher, was mean, and on the playground the other children often laughed at me.

That morning, as Esty and I were passing the old saloon at the edge of town, we saw in the ditch a big pile of chewing gum, still in packs. That was like discovering a gold mine!

A closer look, however, showed that mice had chewed the edges of the gum and ruined it for sale. We sat down, sorted the loot, and found a dozen sticks the mice had missed. Esty and I divided them and put the find in our lunch boxes. We thought, *This is going to be a good day after all.* Esty always called it our "chewing gum day."

Every Monday, Miss Null was especially fierce. She used her ruler to establish justice and secure discipline. On that particular Monday, just before the bell rang, I saw a boy sneak to my desk and quickly switch his reader with mine. Johnny Summet, sitting next to me, saw it. I was too timid to raise a fuss, so Johnny and I looked at the book the boy left on my desk. The page for that day's reading lesson was missing.

As I feared, when class started, Miss Null said, "Levi, you read about the boy and the dog on page eighteen."

I mumbled, "I can't because the page isn't here."

With that, she grabbed her ruler and came toward my desk. "You tore your new book. Now stand up!"

I was speechless with fear, but little Johnny came to my rescue. In his tongue-tied speech, he explained what had happened. I wasn't spanked, but Miss Null didn't do a thing to the guilty boy.

At noon recess I sat down on the top step at the front door to contemplate the new setting. I had my tablet and pencil and was doodling as I tried to balance the events of the morning with the anticipation of the chewing gum when I got home in the evening.

Just as I was beginning to feel good again, one of the big boys grabbed my feet and pulled me, bouncing, down the steps. The boys all laughed as I picked up my tablet and pencil and retreated to my room. When I got there, Miss Null chased me out again. We were supposed to stay out of the room during recess. Monday finally came to an end, as all days must.

The Great World War was then in progress. We heard children singing funny songs about Kaiser Bill getting bullets in his pants. Parents were saying that we had to eat war bread instead of regular white bread. War bread was made with unrefined flour and tasted like wood. Eva said it was nutritious and wholesome, but it made poor apple butter sandwiches.

Miss Null was especially patriotic because, so we heard, her boyfriend was enlisting in the army. She often told us patriotic things that were hard for first-graders to understand but made us feel loyal and brave anyway.

One day she came to school with red eyes and was sniffling in her handkerchief. She seemed confused and called some of the children by wrong names. During noon recess, the little girl who knew everything told us that Miss Null's boyfriend had just been sent overseas.

In the afternoon the teacher put us all at the blackboard to work. She wrote a sentence at the top of the board and told us to copy it. We had to copy it, then erase it, and copy it again—over and over. Then Miss Null went to her desk and laid her head

in her arms. We were on our own.

We copied and erased and copied and erased, and Miss Null never moved. Finally, everybody just stood at the board doing nothing. Things got a little crucial for me. I raised my hand for the bathroom, but Miss Null was in limbo. Just when I got to the point of despair and necessity, I looked down the row of children and saw three puddles on the floor. With great relief I added puddle number four. When the bell rang, Miss Null just got up and, without a word, ran out of the room.

I always walked home with Esty. That evening she was embarrassed. As I walked beside her, the boys began pointing at the wet ring on my pants and made accurate and appropriate remarks about it. After that, Esty would wait for me down in front of Mumaw's Restaurant, a block away. At that time I

began to walk home with Johnny Summet, who lived close to us. We soon became friends.

One time on the way home, he showed me a button on his coat that was coming loose. I said, "You'd better show it to your mama so she can sew it on before it falls off."

He sadly replied, "I can't. My mluver [sic] is dead."

I watched him going down his lane, all the way to his house. I wondered who made supper for him. Tears ran down my cheeks as I walked the rest of the way home.

When I told Mama about it, she somehow missed the emotional part of the story and addressed the matter of the button. "Yes," she said, "if one of your buttons comes loose, be sure to bring it so poor Mama can sew it on again." The words "poor

Mama" struck deeper into my emotions. I pitied her for working so hard and was afraid she would die like little Johnny's "mluver."

During that period I cried sometimes when I was by myself. Another thing that stirred my emotions was the little dried carcass of a kitten that had a long time ago hung itself in a roll of wire. Esty and I found it in one of the farm sheds. She composed an elegy about the poor little kitty crying, and its dear mama looking for it in vain. She would sing it just to make me cry.

One Saturday when we were in the meadow, playing at the creek, she tried the song on me again. That time I hollered, "Oh, shut up!" The elegy had lost its power over me. It was over; it was done.

As if to further establish my new freedom, I took my little boy rag doll, Freddy, which I had along for play, and threw him in the creek. "Swim, Freddie, swim," I shouted. Freddy was stuffed with excelsior. He soon swelled to twice his size, and his contents spilled into the creek. I laughed and grabbed what was left and flung it across the meadow. Somehow, I felt important.

Esty said, "I'm going to tell Mama."

"Go on and be a tattletale," I told her. "I don't care."

I began to enjoy going to school. The boys would get me to join in games at recess. Miss Null began to seem nice even though she wasn't pretty like my other first-grade teacher in Amelia. School was almost over, and the birds were singing in the trees.

25

Emmalene

Emmalene Eshleman owned our farm. We were renting it from her while Papa was looking around to buy a place of our own. Coming in the lane, Emmalene lived in a neat little cottage about a hundred yards from the road, on the left. Next came our farm buildings, on the right.

On down the lane a short way, on the left, was the Pfautz farm. Little red-haired Rufus Pfautz was my summer playmate. The lane ended a little farther at an old abandoned stone quarry. Swallows nested in its rusting derrick and crusher.

Our mailbox wasn't right in front of our house like it had been at Amelia. It was way down by the main road where the lane began. The neighbors' mailboxes were all there, too. Ours was on the right side, and the two others were on separate posts on the left. I thought maybe I would be big enough by now to go down and get the mail.

THIS WAY TO OLD QUARRY PIT

OUTHOUSE

HOUSE

OUTHOUSE
ROSE
BUSH

SHED

EMMALENE
ESHLEMAN'S

BARN

WILLOW

STREAM

BRIDGE

MEADOW

the
Eshleman
Place

MAILBOXS

← LITITZ

ROTHSVILLE →

Soon after we settled in the Eshleman Place, Papa bought a Model T Ford. Automobile talk replaced horse-and-buggy conversation. Now instead of playing with stick horses, I was rolling old tires with Rufus. He brought over two old tires, and we played automobile. We pushed and guided them with short sticks, blowing our horns, "Ah-oogah, Ah-oogah!" My tire was a Ford, and his was a Chevy.

The Pfautzes had a big tobacco field by the lane. We didn't raise tobacco, so I asked Rufus, "Why do you folks grow tobacco?"

He replied, "My daddy told me the only things that use tobacco are people and tobacco worms."

One day I was watching our cow, old Yeloozer, eating grass across the lane from the tobacco field. Rufus and I were talking about tobacco again. I wondered, "Do you think it's really true that animals don't use tobacco, like your dad said?"

"Well," Rufus responded, "let's see if your cow can be fooled into eating some." He fixed a little bit inside a bunch of clover and gave it to the cow. She accepted it, but immediately after the first bite, she spit it out. We tried several times to fool her, with no success.

I summed up the result of our scientific experiment: "Okay, now we know that tobacco is not for cows!"

Our landlady, Emmalene, was a sprightly little widow lady. She was always neatly dressed. Everything about her property looked like Emmalene. The yard reflected Emmalene. Her house with its shuttered windows looked like Emmalene.

The meek little outhouse sat to one side, apologizing for itself. A beautiful rose bush close by helped to divert attention and keep it company.

Emmalene would chase us off her yard if we so much as set one foot on it. She didn't seem to like children. Esty and I felt rejected. Then Esty proposed, "If we decorate her peach tree with flowers, she'll like us."

One day when she was gone, we gathered a lot of wild cornflowers and Queen Anne's lace and hung garlands and chains of flowers all over the tree. Just as we finished, we saw an automobile drop Emmalene at the end of the lane.

Our anticipation of praise was short-lived. She accused us, "You've been trespassing while I was away and vandalizing my tree."

Esty's explanation was to no avail.

"Them's not flowers," she scolded. "Them's weeds. Pull them off and throw them on your side and go on home!"

Sometimes on Sunday afternoon, Emmalene would invite ladies' groups for cookies and lemonade. A table and chairs were arranged on the lawn, and the cookies and lemonade pitcher were covered with napkins, to keep off the flies. Esty and I would sit in our yard and watch the ladies eat cookies and sip lemonade while they laughed and talked.

Beside the path to the outhouse, Emmalene would always place a little table with a basin of water and a towel. From time to time during the afternoon, someone would walk over to look at the "bee-you-tiful" roses and as an afterthought disappear into the outhouse. The basin and towel were discreetly used on the way back to the lawn party.

Emmalene had a pet garden project. She took pride in her special potatoes. They came in three colors: white, blue, and red. She told Papa, "I'll furnish the seed potatoes and the garden space, and we'll divide the crop half and half if you do the work." That was the mutual agreement.

When the crop was harvested, Papa divided the potatoes into two equal piles on the barn floor. Emmalene had first choice. Papa and Brother soon had our pile sorted into large and medium sizes and stored in the cellar. It took Emmalene two days to sort hers. When she was finished, there were six piles on the barn floor. There were large and medium in each of the three colors.

Papa thought that since the potatoes were there so long, she wanted him to bring them to her house. He put all the big ones together and all the medium ones together. He was color-blind and mixed the colors.

She was disgusted. "I worked so blamed hard, and now I have to do it all over."

Papa sent Esty and me over to help her. During our time together, she warmed up to us a little. She asked about school and said, "Years ago, I taught school for a while."

After that she often stood in the yard when the older girls passed by, on the way to the mailbox. She would talk to them about education and advised them to prepare to teach. "You see, I know your father was a schoolteacher, too."

After that she didn't chase us off her yard anymore. Sometimes she even waved at us across the lane.

<u>26</u>

Don't Pass the Elderberry Pie!

The locusts were blooming, and we were walking barefooted. Mama said, "When the locusts bloom, you may shed your shoes for the summer. That's how we did it when I was a little girl." The older people didn't usually go barefooted.

To show our bravery and manhood, we boys would walk over rough places on purpose. Scratches and bandages were the equivalent of knighthood. When Esty picked out smooth places, we called her a sissy.

In our little country church in Virginia, the small children would come to Sunday school in bare feet. It was a spring event when we were allowed to do it. When one of the boys came to church with a band-aged foot, the others gathered around him while he

described his injury. He was a hero.

Now, here in Pennsylvania, I was eager to see all the children in bare feet. I already had some scratches, ensuring me satisfactory recognition. But when I entered the church, I knew something was wrong.

All the children were wearing shiny Sunday shoes! I was visibly barefooted and alone in that style. My face grew red when people looked at me and smiled. The Sunday school teacher acted as though she didn't notice. But some of the kids whispered and pointed at my feet.

After church I slipped out around the back way, passing two old women. One of them noticed me and said to her friend, "*Ei! Er hot ken Schuh* (Oh! He has no shoes)."

The other answered, "*Er is gewiss baarfiessich* (He certainly is barefooted)!"

That's when I began to understand Pennsylvania Dutch. I knew I was not wearing shoes, and I knew I was barefooted. We also found out that here everyone, including children, wore "Sunday shoes" to church even in summertime.

Granny's regular home was with Aunt Alice. Since we had lived away so long, she was glad to come and stay with us for awhile. Mama was getting her room ready. Because we needed an extra mattress, we decided to move the mattress from Brother's and my room and to make a cornhusk mattress for us.

We boys were pleased with that idea. Brother and I had slept on cornhusk mattresses before and liked the rustling sound when we moved around.

Since fresh cornhusks were not available, Papa

took me along to a field near the road where some last year's corn fodder was stacked along a fence. Papa spread some of the fodder on the ground to see if he could find any suitable cornhusks. He said, "It's just as I thought: the husks are too dry and brittle."

We had just finished stacking the fodder back against the fence when we saw a man approaching us from the lane. He told Papa, "I'm an army recruiter officer, and so I am checking out newcomers in the area."

Papa said, "I'm too old, and I have six children."

The man said, "I can see that what you say is probably true, but I have to report it anyway." He took down information about Papa and Mama, and the names and ages of all the children. As he left, he said a pleasant "Good day."

Papa commented to me, "That reminds me of my army days. We had to make so many reports."

Close by along the fence there were a lot of bushes full of little berries. Papa said, "Here are some nice elderberries, but they aren't ripe yet. They're good for pies, but we can eat them raw, too."

Then Papa took out his pocketknife and cut off a short length of stem. He showed me the pith inside the stem and explained, "I used to make whistles and squirt guns out of elderberry stems when I was a boy, like this." As I watched, he made a little whistle for me.

Back at the house, Papa told Mama, "We'll have to buy a mattress for Granny's room. We can't find any good cornhusks."

When he related about the recruiter, Mama was concerned. "They can't get you now, can they, Henry?"

"Oh, no. I've served my time, and I'm too old now, anyhow." He put her mind to rest and took the empty bags back to the barn.

I told Mama about the elderberries and that Papa said they made good pies. When I told Brother about the elderberry whistles and squirt guns, he began making some. He showed Papa some real works of elderberry art in whistles and squirt guns. But Papa said Brother was getting too old for playthings since he was eleven years old.

Esty and I watched the elderberries. When they were ripe, we gathered a bucketful. While we were picking them, we ate so many that we became half sick. We grew to hate elderberries.

Mama was so glad Papa said her elderberry pies were good. She served them every day during the season. Only years later did Papa say that he never liked elderberry pies. He only ate them to please Mama. At that same time, he found out that none of us, including Mama, liked them either. She only made them because he said they made good pies.

Granny came as scheduled. She was a prim little woman, always neatly combed and dressed. Her room was her sanctuary and off-limits to all except Mama. We had furnished her room with a bed, a chest of drawers, a dresser, and a chair. The dresser accessories were a comb and brush, a hand mirror, and a celluloid hair receiver.

A hair receiver, found on most women's dressers at that time, was a container about three inches high and three inches in diameter. There was a round opening in its removable top to receive hair from combs and brushes.

When it was full, the contents were ordinarily consigned to the stove. But we were warned never, not ever, to burn *Granny's* hair. She was superstitious and said, "If my hair is burned, it will make my head ache." So we took her hair to the garden and covered it with dirt.

Granny always slept a little late, so Mama kept her plate ready and her breakfast warm. There was a regular ritual. Mama would pour the coffee in Granny's special cup with its deep matching saucer. Granny would sit down and pour some coffee into the saucer to cool while Mama brought her breakfast. After Mama sat down to keep her company, Granny would pray a blessing in a stage whisper, her German rising and falling. We could distinguish words such as *"Gsundheit* (health)." She finally closed the prayers with an audible "Amen."

The coffee in the saucer was now cool enough for her to sip, and she did so with rippling slurps. Now was the time for chitchat and news. Mama said a girl they knew was getting married. Granny wondered about the boy. *"Iss er gute gfixed* (is he well off)?"

Mama replied, *"Ya, er hut en Haus* (yes, he has a house)."

"Iss es gute gbaute (is it built well)?"

"Ya, es hut en Shindeldach (yes, it has a shingle roof)."

After some thought, Granny asked, *"Iss er bei die Gmee* (does he belong to the church)?"

"Ya, ich denk er geht verleicht zu Groffdale (yes, I think perhaps he goes to Groffdale)."

Granny was always saying, *"Was iss, was iss* (what's that)?" and inserting herself into whatever was going on. As a result, when I became too nosy, the others in our family began to call me "*glee was iss, was iss* (little what's that)."

One time Eva and Helen saw Granny watching them from the porch as they were raking in the yard. So for fun, they acted like they were fighting each other. As expected, Granny went in the house to tell Mama. But not as expected, Mama came out and gave them each several resounding whacks.

They told Mama, "We were just fooling Grandma."

"Well, then I should have given you a few more whacks!"

Later Eva reported to us three younger children, "We could see that Mama was trying not to laugh."

Grandma also held stock in *Braucherei,* a common practice and belief among some older people. Often called "powwowing," it is different from Native American ceremonies. Using old European customs, a person would *brauche* by reciting a few words, often from Scripture, hoping God would heal or relieve pain. Certain actions might go along with the words.

"It's right because *es tut* (it works)," Grandma told Papa.

Papa figured it was superstition and said, "Not everything that works is right."

Mama never took up the matter with Grandma about her numerous signs and portents.

Having Grandma around was interesting and mostly pleasant. Grandpa had left her a comfortable income. She made charitable donations and gave gifts to her children. She also watched little Mary

Elizabeth, who was in her crawling stage.

Toward evening, after an especially pleasant summer day, Mama and Granny were in trivial conversation when Mama said, "Mom, did you have your headache again today?"

"*Nee, ich hab die ganz Daag recht gut gschpiert* (no, I've felt real good all day)."

Mama said, "*Ich hab yuscht gewunnert. Ich hab ebbes vun deins Haar im Offe gschteckt* (I just wondered. I stuck some of your hair in the stove)."

Granny quietly put her hand on her forehead. "*Nee, es dut net weh* (no, it doesn't hurt)."

27

How, What, When, and Where?

Our lease on Emmalene Eshleman's farm was running out. We would soon be moving again. Where would it be this time? Papa said, "We won't worry. Everything will work out."

Granny was saying, "I want to move back to my *Schtibbche* (little room) at Alice's," the home of her daughter, my aunt. "I want you to know that it isn't because I don't like you all." Her positive-sounding discussions were stressed with words like *verschteh* (understand), *gewiss* (for sure), and *verhafdich* (truthfully).

School was out. We children wondered, "Will we be changing schools again?"

Papa told us, "I'm looking for a place somewhere near Lititz that we could afford to buy."

Mama said, "It's easy to say what we want to do.

But how will we do that? When I was a little girl in school, my teacher gave us four important words to think about: *how, what, when,* and *where.*"

Papa smiled and gave us a maxim, "Wait with patience."

So we all waited, but patience wasn't easy.

I hoped we would get a place that had possums.

What happened next? The story will continue in book two.

The Author

Levi B. Weber, Newport News, Virginia, is a retired building contractor, real estate developer, and broker. In the *Possum Hollow* books, he tells of his birth in 1911 and his growing-up years in Virginia and Pennsylvania.

During the Great Depression, Weber held jobs on farms, in a commercial greenhouse, and at a dairy. He bought two acres of forest, harvested the timber, and built a four-bedroom house. In 1939 he and his bride, June E. Burkholder, moved in. They have three children.

After World War II, Weber went into contracting, building, and land development. His company built houses around Old Williamsburg, some for employees of Colonial Williamsburg, and notably for Ivor Nöel Hume, head archaeologist at Colonial Williamsburg.

While developing Denbigh Plantation, the remnant of a historic estate on the banks of the James River, Weber's company discovered the remains of the old Mathews Manor, dating back to 1620. Mr.

Nöel Hume conducted the research and cataloging of the artifacts. For Weber's role in locating, studying, protecting, and preserving Mathews Manor, the American Association for State and Local History gave Weber an Award of Merit.

In 1962 he began as a real estate broker. Eventually Weber retired from building and later from realty work. He gives talks about Denbigh Plantation and Mathews Manor at libraries and local historical organizations. He took a writing course at the College of William and Mary, and writes and publishes stories.

Levi and June are members of the Warwick River Mennonite Church. He has been teaching Sunday school for more than fifty years. Weber has served in leading positions in the congregation and in the conference. For eighteen years, he produced the *Rock of Ages* radio broadcast and directed the chorus for it.

Weber has taught teacher-training courses, given talks about Mennonites, and served on the boards of Eastern Mennonite College and Mennonite Economic Development Associates (MEDA). For MEDA, he made five trips to Africa. Weber was a charter member of the Mennonite Christian Leadership Foundation.

He has been active as a board member of the Mennowood Retirement Community and was president during construction of the seventy-room assisted-living addition. In the 1990s, Weber was part of a volunteer task force shaping a Framework for the Future, for the Newport News Planning Commission.

Weber enjoys researching his Swiss-German family background, translating Pennsylvania German pastoral letters of the 1800s, and studying the history and archaeology of old plantations. Earlier he played golf and flew small aircraft. As a passenger with another pilot, he survived a crash in the Virginia mountains and has lived to tell his tales, for the enjoyment of readers.